Attercliffe

a wander up the 'cliffe

by Michael Liversidge

Text copyright 2001 © Michael Liversidge

Photographic copyright © Michael Liversidge, Jack Wrigley, David Richardson Collection

ISBN 0 9534267-5-0

1st reprint 2002 by Pickard Publishing

Published & Printed by Pickard Publishing

11 Riverside Park

Sheaf Gardens

Sheffield S2 4BB

Telephone 0114 275 7222 or 275 7444

contents

attercliffe common:

attercliffe road

attercliffe common ends at weedon street
and starts at kirkbridge road

attercliffe road ends at kirkbridge road
and starts at twelve o'clock court

Introduction

Looking through an old Sheffield and Rotherham Kelly's Directory (1957) I found my memory of the Attercliffe I knew fading away. I looked at the names of shops in which I had been many times, cinemas I almost lived in, public houses regularly visited and I genuinely struggled to recall them in my mind's eye. At this point I visited my parent's house and purloined all their pictures of myself as a child, plus others of family and friends, some with old Attercliffe looming grimly in the background.

With these images and those supplied by a friend, **Jack Wrigley**, and others from the **David Richardson Collection**, I hope, in this book, to conjure up memories of what Attercliffe was to me from the late 1940s to its 1980s demise... ...with odd glimpses of its rise from the ashes.

The pictures, which span about 30 years, will stand on their own merits, I will just offer you my own personal recollections of friends, family and my views of Attercliffe. I don't for one second think I can capture the formula of what made Attercliffe such a special place in so many hearts, or even with the aid of the photographs capture the sheer volume of people on the streets day and night. See what you think!

Being born (1949) on the 'cliffe (302 Attercliffe Common to be precise) and living and working in that area for 25 years I have my own perspective on life around Attercliffe from the fifties until the mid 1970s. From leaving Coleridge Road School in 1964 I worked at two printing companies, Elias Bradbury and Fred Mellings situated on Attercliffe Road and Zion Lane respectively.

I don't want to look at Attercliffe through rose tinted glasses; the cramped housing facilities, the shocking noise from the steam hammers, 24 hours a day, the massive volume of dirt the factories spewed out on to the Attercliffe streets did not make it the most pleasant place to be raised.

The local football teams I played for, in my teens, had one player crushed, burned to death, a player manager lost half his hand and a teammate and close friend's father was killed in one of those big black steel firms, that seemed to be at the end of every Attercliffe street. Dangerous places.

When people talk of the 'cliffe these things should not be forgotten.

Though, when I look back, I don't seem to recall a vision of these serious health threatening issues. What I remember are happy days playing football in the rec (Carbrook Recreation ground), shopping with my mother in the many and varied outlets along the main thoroughfare, swimming (wading) in the Attercliffe baths, visiting one of the four cinemas on offer, drinking the gorgeous warm, never hot, vimto from one of the many herbalist along the 'cliffe or the once a year (saved for) trip to the Attercliffe Palace of Variety, and when older drinking in the many, many pubs and clubs along Attercliffe Common and Attercliffe Road.

So, maybe just a glimpse through a slightly rose tinted monocle!!

ATTERCLIFFE COMMON

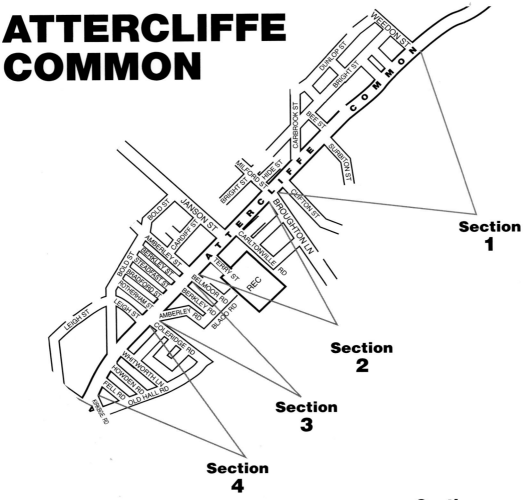

Section 1

Section 2

Section 3

Section 4

ATTERCLIFFE ROAD

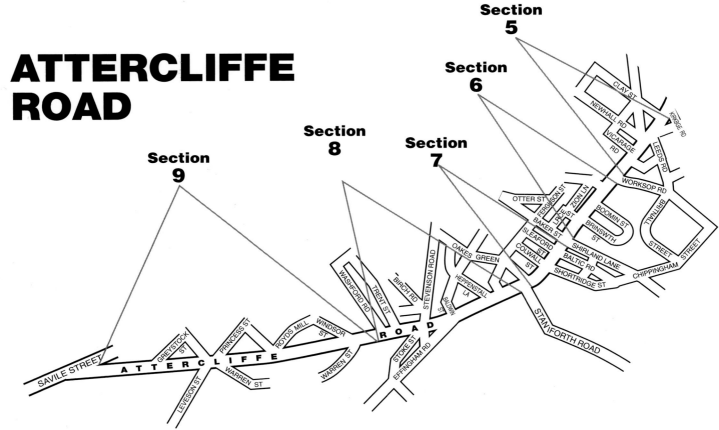

Section 5

Section 6

Section 7

Section 8

Section 9

Weedon Street to **Broughton Lane**

Attercliffe Common, technically speaking ends at the corner of Weedon Street. Therefore in this book we are really wandering back up the 'cliffe.

The area at the top of Weedon Street, where it joins Attercliffe Common, was noted for the number of public houses. On one side of the Common **The Commercial**,* **The Royal Hotel**, **The Union** and opposite the **Tinsley Hotel**, **The Burns Hotels*** were all within about eighty yards of each other.

The Commercial on the corner of Weedon Street was a large Wards Brewery public house which was a popular place for the local darts fanatics in the sixties and seventies. In fact the Wards Breweries Darts Finals were held there on many occasions. One landlord, Reg Williams, served the pub faithfully from leaving the Marines in 1952 and remained for thirty eight years behind the Commercial bar until he retired in 1990. At the time of going to press the Commercial is once again boarded up.

The Commercial Hotel

The Union, a small little pub was tucked between Foxs' and, I think, a furniture shop and was one of the first pubs to be demolished in the earlier slum clearance of Attercliffe.

The Tinsley Hotel was a pub I only visited once, in the summer of 1969, we were out on someone's bachelor party. All I can recall is sitting, with my drink, on a staircase near to the bar. I believe the Tinsley Hotel closed in the very early seventies.

I know very little about the Burns Hotel. I think it was closed before my introduction to public houses. So it was probably closed in the early 1960s. The address was 2 Sheffield Road.

The Royal Hotel

The Royal Hotel, stood on the corner of Mons Street, formerly Blucher Street, and Attercliffe Common. The street named Blucher, after the saviour of the British Army in 1815 at Waterloo, was renamed when a local tale of bravery came along during the First World War, after the battle of Mons, where a large number of young men from the Sheffield area lost their lives.

The street was renamed in 1916.

The Burns Hotel and the Commercial were on Sheffield Road, not Attercliffe Common

The shops in this area were mainly situated on the right hand side heading up Attercliffe. These included, on the corner of Weedon Street and Attercliffe Common, at **679 Mrs Sarah Devonshires' chip shop**. Number **641 Triumph Libraries, 643 Miss G. Francis** Ladies Hairdresser and at **645-647 L F Fox's**,

The Pheasant Inn with the partly demolished AEI in the background

I remember Fox's selling clothes and camping gear etc, but in one old directory of 1957, it mentions Fox's as a jewellers!

The left hand side of the lower Common was predominantly steel works, **Tinsley Wire Industries Ltd (TWIL), Amalgamated Electrical Industries (AEI)** with just the aforementioned Tinsley Hotel and Burns Hotel to separate them. Part of the AEI was built on the Pheasant Recreation Ground, where fairs and circuses would be held on regular occasions in the fifties.

The Pheasant Public House at 436 Attercliffe Common was one of the few pubs in this area to house a full size snooker table. This is another pub that has gone the distance and is still trading, albeit under a new, slightly silly, name, the **Stumble Inn**..

The Interior of the Pheasant Inn snooker room. Note the sink in the corner

The Pheasant was next to the Carbrook Church, **St Bartholemews**. My parents were married here, as were many other members of my family. Others were Christened and some, sadly, had their funeral services held here.

This Church, which until I started this book, I never knew was called St Bartholemews, also housed the local Scouts and Cubs troops a couple of nights a week. I believe it was closed for about a year and then demolished in the early 1960s.

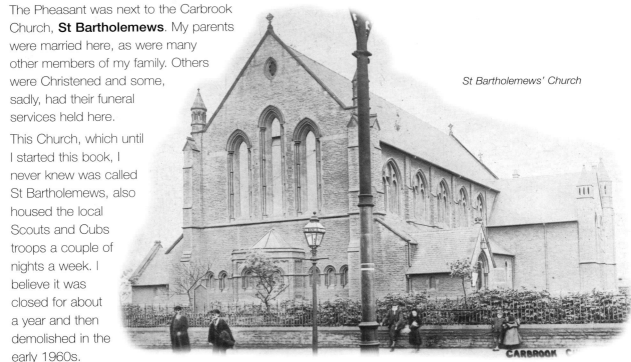
St Bartholemews' Church

The Carbrook Hall

The Carbrook Hall is at number **537** Attercliffe Common and is reputedly the most haunted pub in Sheffield. It has a sign outside that states this, so it must be true! The word Carbrook is said to be a Saxon name meaning stream.

It was first mentioned in about 1170 when it was said to be the home of the Blunt family. Some four hundred years later, during the reign of Elizabeth I, we find it under the control of a Richard Fenton and then the Bright family, and by 1637 the Hall was owned by John Bright, who fought, with some distinction alongside Oliver Cromwell, during the English Civil War, 1642-1649. Bright was appointed Governor of the Sheffield Castle, still standing at that time, after the Roundheads had taken it from Royalists control in 1644. He left the army as a colonel in 1650, and was made a baronet by Charles II. He died in 1688. From this point onwards the Hall passed down through the centuries until in the 19th century it became the Common Beer House and since then it has stayed a public house. The parlour is the central attraction, but I am led to believe the Black Oak room upstairs, which is not open to the public is the better of the two rooms. Treat yourself and go down Attercliffe and see the Jacobean

Carbrook Hall Jacobean fireplace and oak panelling

fireplace, Elizabethan plastering and oak panelling, it is well worth the visit.

It is now a very cosmopolitan pub, with its outdoor seating combined with umbrella style heaters, good food and a pleasant atmosphere making this pub, possibly, the best on Attercliffe.

Further up the Common at number **469** was **The National Union of General & Municipal Workers**. **J A Fearns & Son** Motor Engineers was at number **443** on the lower corner of Carbrook Street and Attercliffe.

There were a number of public houses on Carbrook Street, the **British Oak** and **New Inn**. The latter is still standing, but has not served beer in over 20 years and is now a company canteen or rest room. The **White Horse**, sited on the Corner of Dunlop Street, and the **Industry** which was on Dunlop Street.

A good friend of mine, Walt Osguthorpe was landlord of this establishment in the sixties.

The Industry

The New Inn

On the upper corner at number **1 Carbrook Street** was **The Excelsior** a wonderful little Wards public house where I spent many a happy night. For a period of time in the early 1970s a workmate of mine Roger Pryor and his wife tried their luck at running the Excelsior. He worked during the day at Fred Mellings Printers and helped his spouse in the pub in the evenings. Sadly it did not work out too well and within a year they had both moved on.

The Excelsior

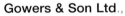

Gowers & Son Ltd., Grocers was next at **439-441** Attercliffe Common. They also had a shop at number **79** which was on the corner with Frank Place.

Then there was **Stamfords Fishing Tackle** shop at **419**, a place where I would go with my good friends Lee Froggatt, Grant Froggatt and Allan Dent to purchase all their angling needs. I would stand there whilst they got their bait, flys, lead shots, floats and whatever else they needed purchased and just think to myself how could anyone work all day in a shop with that awful smell of maggots. I never really got the angling bug other than netting a few sticklebacks from the canal and placing them in a jam jar or does that count? Mind you those sticklebacks were bigger than some of the fish my mates caught, even with all their gear.

*Did you notice the Christian names of the Froggatt brothers, they were named after the two protagonists in the American Civil War, Generals Grant and Lee. Bit of thought went into picking the children's names in the forties.

A little higher on the same side of the Common at number **415** was a hairdressers shop called **My Fair Lady**. In the 50s it was called Cliffe Hairdressers. Nearer to Milford Street **Ethel May Boldock** had two fishmongers shops at numbers **403** and **407** she was a relation of **Horace Boldock** who also owned two fishmongers shops, one on the **Common** at **160** and the other at **551 Attercliffe Road** facing the bottom of Staniforth Road.

At number **401** on the Corner of Milford Street and the Common was **John Thompson** Fruiterer. **Milford Street** itself was a small thoroughfare with two public houses, the **Fitzwilliam** and the **Wentworth House,** a couple of shops, a hairdressers: **Walter Barker**, a grocers: **Harry Duckenfield** and various dwellings, all leading down to the bottom where the English Steel main gates were situated.

The Fitzwilliam Hotel

The Wentworth House Hotel

Things change, the gates at the bottom of the street have led into **English Steel**, **British Steel**, **Avesta** and now **Corus Steel**. The company could well have altered again before this book goes to print!

The Wentworth House is still fighting its corner but the Fitzwilliam is now demolished (that went in the 1980s) and the dwellings are no more.

There is one upside to this tale.

A new public house has been built near to Milford Street.

The Arena Square is a Brewers Fayre family pub, and it is the first public house built on Attercliffe Common for well over 80 years.

The Arena Square

11

Alan Brady (Bug) a friend and team mate with Carbrook United, lived on Milford Street.

In 1968 when Alan was the first of our wee band to get married, at 18 years of age, we started his bachelor night in the Bird in Hand on Broughton Lane and then off to the city centre's Rotherham House on Exchange Street for the remainder of the night.

We knew how to have a good time in those days!

A view of Milford Street looking from the bottom of Broughton Lane in the early 1980s

Allan Dent: (Louie), yours truly and Alan Brady (Bug) on his stag party 1968

Milford Street showing dwellings on the left and the Fitzwilliam and Wentworth House Hotels on the right

Going back across the Common to **No 372** on the corner of Clifton Street was **M Stenton and Co (Sheffield) Ltd**., Ale & Stout Bottlers - Wine and Spirit Merchants. The other corner was taken up by Bob Hewitts, I am sure this was a barbers but in a street directory I have it described as **370 Attercliffe Common, Hewitt Bob,** baker. So when my mother·said go and get the basin cut at Bobs did she know more than she let on? Mind you, he did have a knack of putting the brylcream on with a piping bag!

Clifton Street itself held something of a mystery for us young folks in the fifties. It was said to still have a piece of the gibbet that old Spence Broughton was left hanging from for 20 years. With this piece of information and the supposition that the gibbet could still be seen near Tinsley Locks, I wasted a good few days cum weeks of my life looking for these lumps of wood, to no avail.

I was told the gibbet post was outside the **Yellow Lion** which was at **59 Clifton Street**. As the Yellow Lion had disappeared many years before I can remember, **Mrs Ada Goddard** a grocer was our target for questioning as she was situated at No. 59.

Clifton Street

At **19 Clifton Street** was **G Keen and Sons** Haulage and Carting Contractors. This company also had premises next door to the Bird in Hand public house at **55 Broughton Lane, (Aston Villas)**, now the Carbrook Working Men's Conservative Club and Institute.

Broughton Lane to Belmoor Road

Broughton Lane was named after an inept highwayman called Spence Broughton who in 1791 robbed a mailcoach on Attercliffe Common and who was caught, tried, hung and then had his body gibbeted for 27 years near to the site of his crime, specifically to deter others getting the idea the Royal Mail would be an easy target.

The Spence Broughton story was never relayed to me at school, it was just a story that was in the fabric of Attercliffe life. It did seem though, everybody older than me had seen the gibbet and certain families had a piece or pieces of poor old Broughton's skeleton. No one ever showed these skeletal remains and all the people who saw the gibbet described it to be in slightly different places.

Broughton Lane

Wraggs Builders Merchants at **15/25** Broughton Lane was the first thing you noticed when turning off the cliffe to head up the lane. Broughton Lane, which is only about 200 yards in length, is another area inundated with pubs. On the same side as Wraggs was the Bird in Hand, The Enfield and the Railway and on the opposite side at the bottom was The Broughton Inn.

The **Bird in Hand** at number **49** was a lovely little two roomed public house. This was my first local and I was a regular from the age of 17. Fred Needham, Lee Froggatt, Allan Dent and myself played cards, mainly crib, five or six nights per week in either the dram shop or snug. In addition to this time consuming hobby, Lee, Allan and I also played football for the 'Bird.

Mick, Allan, Fred and Lee 30 years on

Looking down Broughton Lane on to Attercliffe with Wraggs on the right and the Broughton Inn on the left

Every Friday night during the football season we would have our team meeting in the upstairs room, discussing tactics, fundraising and the like. We would then vacate the room at about 8.30pm for some guys who played table tennis. The team, or most of them, then proceeded up Attercliffe Common on to Attercliffe Road and had a half pint in each pub along the route until we reached the Sportsman or the Green Dragon. This is no William Hague story, and we did this regularly. I often wonder how we even managed to play football at all, never mind the very next day!

**Bird in Hand -
1968**
*Back:
Gordon Kaye,
Terry Round,
Mick Liversidge,
Dougie Rose,
Roger Blades,
Dave Walker.
Front:
Brian Kennedy,
Derrick Hindley,
Lee Froggatt,
Brian Thompson,
Grant Froggatt.*

Gordon Kaye, a printer who worked at Hartleys on Attercliffe Road, (pictured on the back row on the extreme left) emigrated along with his family to New Zealand shortly after this photo was taken.

Ray and Mavis Aubrey were the incumbent landlord and landlady of the bird at this time. A very nice couple who tried to keep the pub ticking along with singalong nights, a variety of sports clubs, including football, table tennis, fishing, and the usual pub games. Ray would not allow swearing in the pub if any woman was present. A feat that may not be possible today?

The Bird in Hand closed in the mid eighties.

Next to the Bird in Hand was **Aston Villas** which was owned by **George Keen** Haulage Contractors. Both the Bird in Hand and Aston Villas have now been turned into the **Carbrook Working Men's Conservative Club** who purchased both buildings in the 90s when a compulsory purchase order was placed on their club which stood at 337 Attercliffe Common. The Bird in Hand building was also used as a typesetters, **Forward Processing** in the late 1980s.

*above
Carbrook Conservative Working Men's Club
and right Forward Processing in the late
1980s*

Higher on the same side were a few more dwellings, a fruitshop, another haulage contractors called **William Bradley** at **73/85** situated next to **The Enfield Public House** on the Corner of Broughton Lane and Surbiton Street. The Enfield is still going strong today, and seems to have weathered the recession, unlike most of the pubs down Attercliffe. Next door, across Surbiton Street, stood the **Railway**. This pub has closed and reopened on innumerable occasions, twice when called the Railway, it closed two more times as the **Stadium**, but has now re-opened and is thriving as the **Noose and Gibbet**.

The Noose and Gibbet

*Looking down
Broughton Lane with the
Railway and Enfield in the
foreground and Aston Villas and Bird in Hand in the distance*

From here still walking up
Broughton Lane you would pass more dwellings before
coming across the **Railway Goods Yards**, where every single day you could see the local coal merchants sacking up, the **Railway Cottages** and **Broughton Lane Station**, British Railway (Eastern Region) and of course the **Sheffield to Goole Canal** which ran parallel to the track.

As well as the aforementioned goods yards, railway station and canal there was also the B & C dairy situated on the other side of Broughton Lane. These location were a young person's delight. The canal could be accessed freely, the three others you entered, let's say, not legally. The canal was the most worrying as I could not swim. Swinging across to the other side on ropes attached to bridges, a good idea then, now seems worryingly stupid.

The B&C Co-operative Society took up most of the opposite side of Broughton Lane with its Dairy, bottling plant, garage, stables, boot repair factory, chemist, and coal depot. Campbell Road, Ravensworth Road, and Melville Road all led off Broughton Lane through to Carltonville Road and the only other business on that side of Broughton Lane was **Carbrook Timber Company Limited**.

The Broughton Inn at **343** Attercliffe Common was a Duncan Gilmour public house and was made up of a large concert room and a much smaller offshot room. Gerry Dorsey, better known to you and me as Engelbert Humperdink, served his showbusiness apprenticeship here, charging only about a fiver a night, long before Las Vegas, and a much larger appearance fee, ever beckoned.

The Broughton Inn still going strong in the 1970s

Broughton Inn awaiting demolition mid 1980s

The Broughton was boarded up for a couple of years before eventually being demolished in the mid eighties.

The Sheffield Arena car park now occupies the land on which the Broughton Inn once stood.

Three shops came between the Broughton Inn and Goulder Place, they were **Browns** Butchers, later **G Burtons** also a butchers, **Porter** grocers, later a **Sue Ryders** shop, and **Greens** Photographers at **340**, **338** and **336** respectively.
I also remember 336 being a card shop, **Gay** or **Gaye cards** (it wouldn't work now, would it?)

Burtons butchers, a Sue Ryder shop and a motorcycle accessories shop, possibly Syd Smiths.

After Goulder Place came **Syd Smiths** motorcycle accessories shop. I think he grew into a larger business and gained more connecting shops along the way. Twelve more shops were to be found along this stretch before coming to Carltonville Road. I will mention only three of them.

At **326-328 R Whymans** grocers, noted for the best confectionery in Sheffield (not an exaggeration). My mother used to take me to Whymans on Saturday mornings to buy the confectionery for the family and invariably I would beg a vanilla slice to be eaten walking back up the 'cliffe.

At the side of Whymans was the gennel which ran up to the back of the shops and on to Clarefield Road.

Syd Smiths motor cycle shops, an alarm shop and the gennel just before Whymans

At **302**, was **Carrigans Pet Stores**, which was owned by my aunt Muriel's father. She along with my uncle, Harry Liversidge, lived with their four children Barry, Christine, David and Brian in the premises behind and above this shop.

I knew this house for I was born and lived there the first three years of my life.

Born in a pet shop, I ask you.

The back yards and storage rooms of all these shops were on Clarefield Road.

The third shop is **Cosy Furnishings** at **292-298**. My mother and father bought their furniture on tick, (hire purchase), from here just after they were married. I am sure we were still making payment when the furniture was thrown on the bonfire and by then I was about ten.

Clarefield Road which housed the back yards of 328 to 290 Attercliffe Common, including Cosy Furnishings, as you will note from the presence of their delivery van.

Now that was costly furniture or, heaven forbid, my parents dodged a few of the payments.

Back across the road to the corner of Milford Street and Attercliffe Common, at **No. 389**, was **D. Hobsons** Refreshments Rooms, doesn't that sound grand? It was later to be known as **Mrs P Roddis** Refreshment Rooms. Next door at **385-387** was **C H Hallatts** Chemist, **383 Marvel Cleaners** and ten more businesses including the **Carbrook Post Office** before we come to the **Carbrook Working Men's Conservative Club** at **337.** My childhood friend Paul Smedley's mother and father were longtime members of this club. When the annual club outing came around they invariably took me along with them for the daytrip to Mablethorpe. Now a free trip to the seaside and five bob spending money was as good as it got! Them conservatives knew how to live it up. You only got half a crown spending money with my dad's club, the Moulders **(Foundry Workers Club).**

Carbrook Conservative Working Mens Club

Next door to the club at **No. 333** was **Harry's Hairdressers**. I think Harry moved into this shop sometime around 1955.

When I was about twelve years old I sauntered into Harry's shop clutching a photo of Tony Curtis with a crew cut hairstyle, I said to Harry "I would like my hair cut like that, please". He replied "people with ginger hair look stupid with the crew cut" and promptly put my picture in the waste bin and gave me my usual short back and sides. That one little item aside Harry was a good bloke, he liked to talk more than listen, but it was his shop after all. He had done everything, been everywhere, played for every football team, caught every fish that ever swam and knew absolutely everything about everything. He even knew film stars. Once, when a little older, I confided in him I was meeting a young lady and he even showed me how to put on a tie correctly so it suited the shirt collar I was wearing. His word was gospel.

Many years after I had moved away from Attercliffe I was passing Owlerton Dog Track on the bus and saw Harry coming out (he did like his bet). He still looked as smart and dapper as ever. I wish now that I had got off the bus to chat to him, I would have told him he was right, I tried the crew cut later in my life and it definitely did not suit a ginger.

About nine more businesses were situated between Harry's barbers and Janson Street of which I can only really remember **Booths Newsagents** at **297** and the **Lambpool Hotel** which was **291**. Booths was the shop from which in the early sixties, I ordered all my football monthly's and soccer stars magazines and Mr Booth used to let me run up a rather sizeable debt before finally harassing me for payment. The public house, the Lambpool, was built in around 1870, and as you can gather from its name it provides some evidence of the once rural aspect that used to be Attercliffe in the late 19th century. The pub itself was a small two roomed, Whitbreads house with a central bar and stood on the corner of Attercliffe Common and Janson Street. It finally closed in the early 1990s and was demolished in 1993.

The Lambpool and Booths newsagents

On the other corner of Janson Street heading up Attercliffe at **287-289** was a grocers owned by **Mrs Mary Hardwick** in the fifties and, in the early to mid sixties, **Mrs L Taylor**.

Rileys Electrical, Dr Nimmo, Frank Cutts bookies, **The File Smiths Arms, Mrs Peacocks** grocers shop, and **The Amberley Hotel** were some of the 15 or so businesses between Janson Street and Amberley Street.

The File Smiths Arms, a Stones public house, was situated on the corner of Tuxford Road. Mr Goodchild was the landlord in the late 50s. His daughter, Mary, was in my class at Carbrook Junior School. I only went into the Filesmiths a couple of times, in the mid to late sixties, and I found it dark and depressing, it was not a place I felt like making my regular.

Filesmiths Arms and next door Cutts Bookmakers

Separating the Filesmiths and the Amberley was Mrs Charlotte Peacock's grocery shop. This shop was packed to the rafters with stock or boxes and packages were stacked all around the floor and it only had a small central area where you could get to the counter. It could not hold more than two customers at any one time. Mrs Peacock did not have a liking for young people and as if to reiterate this, she was the only person on the 'Cliffe who sold Black Jacks and Fruit Salads at two for a penny instead of the usual four for a penny - sacrilege.

Years before, this shop was known as the Argentine Beef Company.

The Amberley Hotel was situated on the corner of Attercliffe Common and Amberley Street. The Hotel itself was a large building with three storeys.

The building consisted of a large concert room, where to hear the locals tell, good quality acts, (turns) performed for two or three nights per week throughout the forties, fifties and sixties. It had two smaller rooms, one directly on the corner, the public bar entrance from the Common and entry into the concert room was gained from Amberley Street. The Amberley Hotel was a John Smiths House selling Magnet Ales. At the turn of the century it had livery stables attached to the premises. It was the local to my father Joe Liversidge and my grandfather Richard (Dick) Otley. The Amberley Hotel was closed in the mid 1970s.

The Amberley Hotel, Mrs Peacocks shop, Tuxford Street, Filesmiths Arms

Back across the Common for the Carltonville Road to Belmoor Road stretch. At **288** was **D Berrisfords** Chippy. When I returned to play with my cousins, David and Brian, who I had lived with years before, I used to pass this chippy on my way home. Fishcake in a breadcake, soaked in salt and vinegar, only sixpence, in old money, what a bargain!! Next door at **286** was the **Tuck Shop** owned by Mr Stanley H Sayles, a very tall, thin mustacheoed gentleman, who always wore a short green, smock and who really did have the patience of Job. Being just yards away from a junior and infant school he obviously had to suffer the scathing wit of the kids. How many times should one man have to listen to:

Have you got any penguins, **yes**, *what do you feed them on.*

Have you got any allsorts left **yes**, *that's your fault for buying too many, and so on....*

But he kept smiling through, well I think it was a smile.

Mr Sayles was a very good musician and played in a combo who did the circuit at wedding receptions and other functions where their more restrained sound could be heard and enjoyed with the knowledge that it would never overpower the event. Unlike some of todays DJs who I am sure have only one level on their turntables, unbearably loud.

Between the Tuck Shop and the School at **No. 282** was **Dr Labib Botros's** Surgery. Now Dr Botros was not my doctor but I did spend quite some time in his waiting room. Carbrook United, a football team, I played for, used to meet here once a week under the watchful eye of Scotch Jim, the

The Carbrook United 1966
back:
Tony Lightowler
Alan Hardisty
Mick Liversidge
Allan Dent
Steve Smith
front: Alan Brady
I Mackenner
Roger Blades
Grant Froggatt
Lee Froggatt

manager. Jim lived with his girlfriend, the doctor's receptionist, in the upper rooms and we had team talks and general meetings, in the evenings, downstairs in the waiting room. At the beginning of our first season in a league, Jim had got us in shape for the season, purchased kit, arranged the pitch and picked himself at centre forward. Come the first Saturday of the season and the get together for the big day and no Jim. He had been seen, that morning, in handcuffs being taken away by the police for non payment of maintenance, to his estranged wife and children. We won the game, the replacement centre forward scored three, and we never saw Scotch Jim again.

Next to the doctors was the infant and junior school, **Carbrook Elementary.** In all my six years at this school, Mrs Carr was the head teacher at the Infants, and Miss Middleton was head of the Juniors. Some of the teachers whose classes I attended: Ms Tucker and Ms Rigden, infants. Ms Gillott, Ms Kirkland, Mr Wild, Ms Dobson and Ms Renshaw Juniors.

It has to be said that in Attercliffe schools in the fifties a class of about 35 pupils was the norm and equipment was basic and in some cases woefully insufficient. The teachers, generally, did their upmost, and taught you to the best of their ability. Occasionally you would find a teacher who could hold the class in the palm of his or her hand and make nearly all the lessons seem not only interesting but necessary, then going to school for that term was a joy. One of these teachers in the infants, a lovely lady, Miss Jean Rigden, also taught my son, Mark, at Pye Bank Infants school in the mid 1970s. I attended Carbrook Elementary from 1954 until 1960, before moving on to Coleridge Road School.

Pupils of Carbrook School 1957

Is that you?

The infants school has now been made into the Players Cafe/Bar. I've had the odd pint in the Players and I must admit I feel very comfortable there. I wonder why?

Players Cafe

Looking toward the old school from Janson Street

22

Terry Street, at the side of Carbrook school, had dwellings on only one side. It also had the only public toilet on Attercliffe Common.

Terry Street led up to **Carbrook Recreation Ground,** which was the only place in Attercliffe I can ever recall seeing grass grow. I imagine that you are thinking that is an exaggeration but it is true. You had to go as far away as Tinsley Park Cemetery, Firth Park or High Hazels Park to actually see more than a just few blades growing.

The rec' itself consisted of two tennis courts, a bowling green, a grassless football area, an old people's hut, and the usual swings and roundabouts. It had another entrance which was on Blaco Road. This area is where Attercliffe Bowl is now situated.

Terry Street looking up to Carbrook Rec

Carbrook Recreation Ground 1927

left: Carbrook Rec, 1949, with Blaco Road entrance in background and a beautiful baby boy in the foreground

right: The Rec, 1953 with my mother pushing me on the swings, Manningham Road in background.

23

Ronald Otley, my uncle, and myself standing in front of the park keepers house in Carbrook rec.

Carbrook Recreation Ground was small compared to most parks and recreation ground but it still had its own live on-site park keeper and a couple of assistants would also be there daily.

Back to the bottom of Terry Street and turn left, you came back on to Attercliffe Common, **No 218 Wagstaff** was a wood-working supplies outlet. You could buy all your woodwork supplies from this shop and for the kids he sold balsa wood aeroplane model kits.

Eight more businesses before Belmoor Road, these included **Cutts** grocer at **210**, Frank Cutts was the same man who owned Cutts Turf Accountants shop almost directly opposite across the main Attercliffe thoroughfare. Many a morning I would buy a warm breadcake from Cutts's grocers whilst walking to school instead of having any breakfast. It was easier for me to stay in bed until as late as possible, around 8.40am, and then hastily get ready and pick up my substitute breakfast on the way to Carbrook school, which started at 9am.

Flathers at **208**, was one of about six fish and chip shops on Attercliffe Common and probably the best. They opened five dinnertimes and five nights per week. For some reason no fish and chips could be bought anywhere at all on a Monday dinnertime or on a Wednesday evening. Strange!

Stuarts Barker's birthday party.... I think??? some of the invited are: Janet Smedley, Susan Pearson, Linda Cutts, Paul Smedley, Michael Liversidge and others

Fish and chips was the staple diet for most families in Attercliffe, It was the 1950s fast food of the day, except you invariably had to wait in a long queue, especially when the pubs came out.

Pearsons, at **206**, were chinaware dealers, Susan, their daughter, was a childhood friend.

At **200** was a Dental Practice, **Harry Heathcott**, was the dentist when I first made a visit. I had broken a tooth and was given gas to have it extracted. The next visit was a few years later but this time the practice was run by a **Mr Senior**.

Finally at **198** was **Northern Vision Company Limited**, Television and Radio supplies, which was situated on the corner of Belmoor Road and Attercliffe Common. I remember we bought our first television, a Decca, from them in about 1957. They delivered it to my home at No. 32 Belmoor Road, one Saturday morning and by about five in the afternoon my grandfather, Richard Otley, a pseudo electrician fixed it up, in a fashion. I can clearly remember the first programme I ever saw on our own television, it was Circus Boy.

Some families, on Belmoor Road, had had television for years and I was often to be found in one of these houses, generally the Smedley household where I would hang on for dear life until the children's hour had finished, sometimes whilst they cooked and actually sat down and ate their meal.

belmoor road to coleridge road

After living on Attercliffe Common with my father's brother for about four years we eventually found refuge elsewhere. In the early fifties it was not the easiest of tasks to find council or even rented accommodation.

When my grandmother, Constance Otley, passed away, in 1953 we went to live with my mother's father, my grandfather, Richard Otley, at number **32 Belmoor Road**.

This was supposed to be an improvement, but really moving into a two up two down house where my grandfather, an aunt and an uncle already lived seemed a little like the frying pan and the fire set up to me.

These houses, row upon row of them in Attercliffe, were pretty spartan to say the least: outside toilet, no heating other than the

Richard Otley standing at the bottom of Belmoor Road outside Shentalls grocers

Yorkshire range coal fire and no bathroom. The lack of a bathroom can be pretty embarrassing, to a young boy of 8 or 9, especially when you sit in the old zinc bath in the middle of the kitchen and your mother comes in to pour the hot water in to keep you warm and invariably decides to mash a cup of tea for the family at the same time.

Most of the households on Belmoor Road seemed to be in much the same state as ours. Overcrowded, with other not always immediate members of their family living with them, but it almost went unnoticed as you just got on with life and made the best of what seemed to be the norm.

Belmoor Road itself had about 30 houses on each side and on the odd numbered side there were two cul de sacs, Scofton Place and Thurley Place. These dead ends were the best places to play football when not in the rec. You had a wall at one end which was obviously the goal and not much traffic came on to these places so the only interruptions you suffered were from the occupants if you struck their door or windows.

Two views of Scofton Place

A family who had more space than most were the Smedleys, who lived at 18 Belmoor Road. Betsy and George, with son Paul and daughter Janet, only four to a household, wow. Paul, or as I knew him Smegs, was my best friend almost from the day I moved into the road. For about 9 years until we moved to senior school we were almost inseparable, a good mate. I don't remember too much about his parents, but I do recall that his dad, George was a rear gunner in Avro Lancasters during World War Two.

Next door to my grandfather's, at number 34 Mrs Wheeler, her daughter, Maud, was married to Frank Cutts. Frank owned the grocers and bookmakers on the Common.

Me and Paul Smedley (Smegs) on Belmoor Road

I used to carry coal up from Mrs Wheeler's cellar, two or three buckets at a time, and leave them at the top of the cellar head so she could use it at her leisure. The payment for this chore was a tanner (sixpence) or 15 minutes on her piano. She was quite deaf so she did not mind too much, but the neighbours on the street were never too amused.

The houses on Belmoor Road all had rear entrances into back yards. These yards held six houses and could also be accessed by an entry/gennel. Nearly all the walls which separated these yards would have either painted or chalked upon them a set of goal post and/or cricket stumps. Even in these little cramped back yards, sport was still keenly played. In fact, Mrs Wheeler's grandson in-law, a chap named Roy Ellis, who was a semi-professional footballer with Rochdale, used to give the eager young boys, myself included, tips on control, heading and shooting.

Unfortunately, the small size of these yards created its own problems. Your parents would say go in the back yard and play, but if you struck a window or door or even worse cracked or broke a window the neighbours would complain that the kids should be in the rec and not playing in their yard.

Paul Smedley, Linda Cutts, and Michael Liversidge in 1955 Linda was the great granddaughter of Mrs Wheeler, whose house we are standing outside

Ron Otley in the mid 1950s. As you can see in the background, Brown Baileys was being extended.

Brown Baileys, outside toilets, backs of the Berkley Street houses and a wall walker

As I have stated before we did live in cramped and unhygenic surroundings. I realised, later, that I had never seen true white clothes until I had moved away from Attercliffe. My mother hung washing out and it invariably came back in looking dirtier that when it went out. I used to be perturbed by this, so goodness knows how my mother coped. I also remember at bedtime, after playing football in the rec, I had to wash my feet thoroughly. I took my socks off and there was a black ring around the ankle almost like a second sock. Sad to say some nights she would say "have you washed yet" and I would reply "Yes mom" and proceeded to climb into bed, unwashed. I somehow thought that she wouldn't notice, Silly.

At the upper end of Belmoor Road at 64 on the corner with Blaco Road, **Bullens** grocers shop, the Aladdin's cave of all grocers shops. You could go to Bullens and get anything you desired at any time of the day.

A derelict Belmoor Road in 1970s

Blaco Road ran parallel with Attercliffe Common along the top of Berkley Road and Amberley Road and had an entrance into Carbrook rec.

At the other side running the length of Blaco Road was Brown Baileys steel works, this structure loomed large over a big part of Attercliffe. Both my grandfather and uncle worked at Brown Baileys in the 1950 and 1960s.

Looking up Belmoor Road, Thurley Place and Blaco Road can be seen leading off

Brown Bailey on the right of Blaco Road and in the distance the entrance to Carbrook Rec

At the corner of Belmoor Road and Attercliffe Common was **John Shentalls Ltd** at **194**. This was a grocers which I don't really recall too much about. What I can bring to mind is that it was larger and cleaner than most shops in this area. My other recollection of Shentalls is of a lady who worked there who was murdered. When I was about nine there was a rumour that someone who worked at Shentalls had had their throat cut. Now I do not know if the grisly details are correct, but I do know that an assistant from this shop was definitely murdered.

Number **192** was **Rutherford**, a bakers. Mister Rutherford prepared all the shop's baked goods in their back yard bakery and the lovely smell of freshly

Shops between Belmoor Road and Berkley Road:
Shentalls, Rutherfords bakers, Ludbrooks hairdressers, Beadmans drapers,
Austwicks fish and chip shop, later Wilsons

made bread is an aroma you never seem to come across now, not even in the larger supermarkets who bake in house. A hairdressers and a drapers came next, I did not have too much interest in these shops. I think, though, at one stage one of the premises was a grocers of some sort, because I do recall it being called locally the "egg shop".

Next was **Austwicks** chippy and later in the sixties **Wilsons**, at **186 Attercliffe Common**. After the chipshop there was a grocers, and on the corner of Berkley Road was a pawnbrokers, Taylors. The "Pop shop" was a place my mother worked at in the late 1940s and early 1950s and it was later owned by a Mrs Gladys Parkin who had it through to the late 1950s. This premises was demolished and was made into a car sales lot.

On Berkley Road itself I remember a few families, the Brearleys, who had a son called Peter, ginger haired lad always whistling or singing, strange the things you recall.

Then there was Mrs Levesley who lived with her two sons Colin and Jeff. Colin was one of our little group of about eight friends. At his house we could have the luxury of a room to ourselves. We would play cards into the early hours. The benefit of this was that the under age members of our group could have a drink. We invariably had to send Lee Froggatt to the off licence, because he looked 10 years older than the rest of us, he shaved twice a day from being about thirteen. We drank Long Life canned beer, this came with its own opener, a dangerously sharp piece of metal to pierce two holes in the top of the can.

The other family I remember was the Dunwells. About three houses were occupied by members of this family. Tragically, Anne Dunwell who was roughly the same age as myself, was brutally murdered on a visit to see a member of her family who lived in the Maltby area. To my knowledge no one has ever been brought to justice for this terrible crime.

On the other corner of Berkley Road was **Nelsons Newsagents**, at **178 Attercliffe Common**. I bought many items from this shop, which, if I had the foresight to have kept, would now be worth a small fortune.

My uncle, Ron Otley, started buying me colour American comics in about 1954. From that point onwards I collected all the titles I could lay my hands on: Superman, Batman, Superboy, Worlds Finest, Justice League of America which were all DC Comic titles. They issued 7 or 8 titles a month all through the 1950 and early 1960s. I eventually finished in the mid sixties with almost 1000 issues. I also collected every vehicle of the matchbox series to be issued, priced I think at £0-1s-3d or £0-1s-6d each. I had a vast collection of American comics, as stated, and the full set of boxed matchbox toys. I was a bit of a wheeler dealer in those days and swopped some of the comics for a set of topical times football annuals and the matchbox cars for football boots and a football. The kid who exchanged my comics for footy annuals lived in Dore, the rich get richer and the thick get thicker!!!!

Attercliffe Common; the lorry is parallel with Berkley Road, Nelsons Newsagents stands on the corner. Dubarrys, Sheffield Gown shop and Jackie Travis Tailors are some of the businesses that are on view

Around this next area from Nelson's Corner up to Coleridge Road I seem to remember **Jackie Travis** having a couple of tailor's shops. He also had at least one shop on the opposite side of the Common, between Amberley Street and Berkley Street. Mr Travis, if memory serves me correctly, also bought the Embassy Ballroom, on Mansfield Road, which he owned for some considerable time.

A few doors away at **166-172** was **Dubarry Gowns**, this was a shop where my mother regularly used to "lay things away". In other words they made her pay for an item, in full, before she got her hands on it. **Jepsons** fruitshop, followed at **164,** the owner, Ethel Jepson, I am sure never used a lightbulb in all the time I lived near to this shop. It was the darkest retail outlet I have ever been in and as a young child I genuinely feared going into her fruitshop, even when accompanied by my mother.

Another eleven businesses were to be found before Coleridge Road. Of these, I only really remember a few, **Hinchcliffes** shoe and boot repairers at **160**, at **144, Fukes** a tripe shop, from which my father and grandfather made me fetch their orders of tripe, bag, and cow heel, even though I begged them not to send me. Just the sight of tripe still makes me feel ill. **Ransomes**, was a tobacconist at **134**, from whom I remember my friends buying 5 woodbines and 5 matches for about a tanner. A bakers shop somewhere along here was owned by a lady with the unusual name of Obelinde Wilson. I also think there was a fish and chip shop in this block of shops. Along this stretch, in the late fifties or early sixties, there was a jewellers-watch repairers, the owner's name was Mr Whiting.

The Bombay Cafe on the corner of Attercliffe Common and Amberley Road

On the corner with Amberley Road and Coleridge Road stood the **Continental Cafe**, later the **Bombay Cafe**, and, even later, the Bow Vaa Continental Restaurant. This was an establishment I never entered, but I spent many a Friday and Saturday night hanging around waiting for the balloon to go up (a fight to start). It has to be said that at times racial tension caused a certain amount of the problems in and around this cafe and many a fracas was to be viewed, generally on a weekend night. We used to sit in the cars on the opposite side of the Common, see page 31, so we had an almost perfect view of any trouble that would start.

On one occasion we were witness to a fight that must have been going for a full ten minutes before the police arrived. Rather strange when you think the police station was only about 250 yards away. During this particular melee a participant had his ear bitten off. On another occasion we saw a man come out of the Cafe holding his stomach, blood spreading on his white shirt, he had been stabbed.

Halcyon days....

The Cafe was only matched for trouble by the Dog and Partridge, much higher up on Attercliffe Road near to the bottom of Staniforth Road, also noted for its Saturday night bust ups.

There were other cafes and restaurants on Attercliffe, indeed other Asian cafes and restaurants, but none of those seemed such a magnet for trouble as did the old Continental.

To cover the equivalent area from Belmoor Road to Coleridge Road on the other side of Attercliffe Common we go from Amberley Street to Leigh Street.

At the corner of Amberley Street, **215** Attercliffe Common was **Hughes's** fruitshop, **213**, **Dewhursts** butchers, **205**, **Frank Dinittos** jewellers, **203**, **Savages** musical instrument sellers and tuners and on the corner of Berkley Street at **201**, **Pioneer** Launderette. I recall washing the football team's kit in this launderette every Monday evening. One season one of Carbrook United's players, Roger Blades, won some money on the football pools and very generously bought a new team strip. It was candy striped, thin red and large white stripes. We played one game looking superb. I washed the kit, the colours ran and we played the rest of the season in a slightly effeminate flamingo pink football strip.

To my knowledge between Berkley Street and Steadfast Street there were only two businesses. The Brightside and Carbrook Co-operative took up the equivilant of about three premises and on the corner with Steadfast Street was a secondhand car sales lot, belonging to G Askham.

The Fruitshop, corner of Attercliffe Common and Amberley Street

I don't remember much about the co-op shop but I do have fond memories of the car lot. There was a small wall all the way around this lot and a gate on the back. No one could steal any of the vehicles, so they never locked the cars. In the evenings when it rained or we needed to eat our fish and chips in comfort our little group would invariably sit in the 'poshest' cars on the lot.

The other corner of Steadfast Street had **Lamings**, bakers at **181**, which was one of five businesses before Bradford Street. Two butcher's, **Olivers**, and **Vessey's** pork shop, **Martins** cleaners and a **beer off shop** on the corner of Bradford Street made up the five. The Beer Off shop was owned by a very tall gentleman whose name I am almost certain was Cornelius Caine, who always wore a long brown smock. Years later Lamings shop became a Secondhand Shop (swop shop), pictured left.

Second hand shop at the corner of Attercliffe Common and Steadfast Street

Hardisty's shop, c1965 at the bottom of Bradford Street looking up towards the cliffe

Bradford Street was just another one of the many thoroughfares leading off the 'cliffe. My knowledge of this street was gained from regular visits to see my friends Allan Dent and Alan Hardisty. The Hardisty family owned the shop (beer-off) at the 'bottom' which can just to be seen in the left hand side of the picture. Allan Dent's father would send us for a Jug of Ale from Hardisty's beer off before we used to head out for a night of snooker or a visit to the cinema.

Back up on Attercliffe Common, four businesses were to be found between **Bradford Street** and **Rotherham Street**, at **169**, **Bakers**, Ironmongers, **167**, **Valentines**, teenage separates, **165**, **Boldocks** fishmongers and at **163**, **Quick Press Limited** cleaners.

On the other corner of Rotherham Street was the **National Provincial Bank** at **145** Attercliffe Common. I occasionally used to play in the Bank, after business, at night. The caretaker was a Mr Bailey and his son, Paul, was one of our happy little band, so occasionally, after closing, we had the run of the bank. They had a big black aggressive guard dog, I think it was called, Blackie, original!

Still heading up Attercliffe Common, next door to the bank there was a greengrocers, **139/141 Alfred Robinson**, and finally at the corner of Leigh Street was **Herbert Kirkups** at **137**. Mr Kirkup's shop stocked everything needed to repair or maintain your home. Mats, mops, buckets, tools and ladders, with almost everything hung outside the premises. I often wondered how he got everything back inside, because upon entering his shop there seemed only a small, central, standing area, perhaps Kirkup's shop was the Tardis of Attercliffe.

Nat West Bank at the top of Rotherham Street

coleridge road to **kirkbridge road**

Coleridge Road to Whitworth Lane
The Salutation pub, Pavilion picture house, library, bookies, butchers,
ironmongers, herbalist, cleaners, doctors, the Gate pub, and finally a
chip shop - what more could you ever want?

The **Salutation Inn** at **126** Attercliffe Common stood on the corner with Coleridge Road. Set between this cream tiled public house and the Pavilion cinema was **Brashaws Brothers** Newsagents and **Thorp**, dental agents at **124** and **122** respectively. The 'Pav', correct title, **The Attercliffe Pavilion** (Heeley & Amalgamated Cinemas Limited) was possibly the easiest of the four cinemas on the 'Cliffe to enter without paying. A group of us would club together and pay for one individual to enter, he would go in and go straight to the toilets, run up to the fire exit doors, push them open and we would all quietly wait until the lights dimmed and enter, sit separately and watch the film for free. We tried this a few times with 2 or even 3 people and got away with it. But on one fateful occasion, after a few successes, our number grew to about seven participants. Everything went to plan, I was selected to enter legally, always a relief. I paid, went in, sat down and waited for a few minutes, then very noncholantly went to the loo. I looked up and down the corridor, no one to be seen, ran up and opened the door and was very nearly trampled to death by the eager mob. "Weers thah been" was hissed at me as the mob shot past. Being a rather intelligent, budding, criminal I proceeded to close the push bar doors. They did not close, I thought which idiot is still outside trying to get in. He was a big blue clad idiot wearing a strange big helmet. The coppers had been alerted by the cinema staff after they noticed a mob standing at the fire exit door looking furtive. We were caught dead to rights, lights turned on, idiots found, idoits thrown out, idiots threatened with more grief if attempted again and to cap it all this idiot did not get a refund. I personally never tried anything like that again.

Next to the Pav, at **112**, **Buckleys**, was a stationers and small library which loaned books out for a small charge. I also remember buying lead toy soldiers from this shop in the mid fifties, another item that would have been of collectable value now.

The Pavilion

In the sixties, **Ibbotsons** Turf commissioning agent (bookies) was at **106**.

At **100** Attercliffe Common was **Frosts** Ironmongers, **98** a hairdressers, **96 Hartleys** Herbalist the best vimto server in Sheffield, followed by a florists, and at **92 Phoenix** Cleaners. My mother worked at this cleaners for about 5 years through the late fifties and into the sixties. In the school holidays I used to sit on the floor behind the counter and cut the buttons off all the clothes that came in to be cleaned. Not through any mischievous intent, in those days all buttons had to be removed before cleaning could take place. Next door was **Fanes** Hardware shop followed by a Doctors Surgery at **86/88**, Doctors **George Wainwright** and **Colin Gething**. How these two men could be in partnership is beyond my comprehension, Wainwright was superior, gruff, obnoxiously blunt and insulting in the extreme, Dr Gething was mild mannered, compassionate and a seemingly caring man. Unfortunately, you could not pick which doctor to see, if a door was left open by a departing patient and you were next, in you had to go. I

Phoenix Cleaners, looking on to the Common with Leigh Street Chapel in the distance

remember once going with my mother when she went to have her ears syringed. She was hoping Gething would be the one to perform the task. Sadly, Dr Wainwright's door was left ajar and in we went. George said to me, a five year old, "go around the other side and keep an eye on your mother's other ear to see if any liquid comes out". I did as I was bid. My mother later explained it was just a joke by the doctor. Mind you, not many scroungers got on the panel (sick pay cover) with Dr Wainwright on their case. I was told he was an ex field surgeon in the British Army, so he probably felt a cold or a swollen ankle or the like did not really warrant time off work. I saw a few annoyed faces come out of his surgery.

Next at **82** Attercliffe Common was a grocers, **Emery's** and at **82b** was **Caravan Supplies** and timber merchants which used **Court 6** to the side and rear to display their wares. Courts as they were termed were courtyards off the 'cliffe. Some were large areas, including dwellings, as in the case of Court 6 and some were no more than storage areas. A friend and workmate of my father's, Eric Codman, lived in this court 6, which could also be accessed from Swan Street.

On the other side of this court at **76/78** Attercliffe Common was the **Old Gate Inn**, another establishment with a reputation for trouble. That being the case, it was obviously a place I avoided.

Brashaws Newsagents was at **72/74, Goodmans** pastrycook at **70** and at **68 Summerhays** fish and chip shop, which sometime in the 1960s changed ownership to the O'Brien's. This chip shop stood

The Old Gate Inn

on the corner of Attercliffe Common and Whitworth Lane.

On Whitworth Lane itself, at number 40, was the one place in Attercliffe you did not want to pay a visit to, this was the **Attercliffe Police Station**.

Back up to the Common on the corner at number **66** was **Bools**, general dealer. Between Whitworth Lane and Howden Road were nine more businesses, I can name some from the directories of the day but I, personally, can only recall **Caplans** watch repairer at **50**. Some of the others shops were: **62 Thorpe** barbers, **58 Jukes**, earthenware dealer, **54 Race**, tripe dealers. **Howden Road** came next and on its corner was **Michael's** Bargain Furnishings at **42**, followed by six more businesses on this block, **40**, **Huddart**, hardware, **38**, **Rimmington**, hairdressers, **36**, **Caryll**, draper, **34**, **Townsend**, furniture dealer, **32**, **Slacks**, baker and on the corner with Fell Road at **28/30** Attercliffe Common was **George Clark** grocer. Between Fell Road and Kirkbridge Road, at the end of Attercliffe Common stood a further five businesses.

Whitworth Lane with Brown Baileys looming across Old Hall Road.

The corner shop on Fell Road was **Cunninghams**, toy shop at **24**, **Sound**, upholsterers at **22**, **Taylors**, potato crisps, at **20**, this shop was transformed into **Samon's Cafe**, in the sixties. The penultimate shop on the 'cliffe was one of my favourites, **George E. Murat**, cycle agents, at **16/18**, **GEM Stores** to the uninitiated. Old George sold models, toy soldiers, cycles, matchbox and dinky cars almost everything I coveted as a child. Most Saturday mornings my mother and I would catch a bus, alight outside Littlewoods shop and proceed to walk back down Attercliffe toward home. This was my cue to be a good son and suggest I would help carry the shopping. Whilst I was never adverse to going into Littlewoods, Banners, Woolworth and the like it was a little tedious every

Kirkbridge Road

Saturday, but the payoff would come as we crossed Kirkbridge Road back onto the Common and looked in GEM Stores window. I invariably needed some item to develop my collection or a new toy had been placed in some prominent position and it was a must have situation. She fell for it almost every time, spoilt kid or what?

The last establishment on this side of the Common at **12/14** was **P. Ferner & Sons** wholesale tobacconists.

Attercliffe Common comes to an end at Kirkbridge Road.

Sale and Exchange

Crossing over the road and going back to Leigh Street for the last section of Attercliffe Common we find at **135**, **Attercliffe Sale and Exchange** a shop that you could take the items you no longer used and barter a price for anything. The problem was the chap in the shop never, ever needed to buy them. He would say "no, not really I've got plenty of those" or "no, sorry, they just don't sell" and then proceed to offer you, as a favour, a really low price. He knew you were in there to get some cash and it was always hard to say no and walk out still carrying the item, so he had you over a barrel. His shop was followed by four more shops before the Old Burial Ground. A butchers, **Wilks** at **133**, a chemists, **Paddon Watts** at **131**, later **H. S. Allens**, chemists, and at **129** a grocers, **Ms Ruth Law**. The last shop was **Herbert Nuttall**, sports outfitter at **127**.

The **Old Burial Ground** with the **Chapel of Ease** is the last resting place for some of Sheffield's famous historic names. The Chapel of Ease is the oldest known surviving building of old Attercliffe and was originally know as the **Hill Top Chapel** and was built in 1629. It was opened in 1630 and was consecrated in 1636. Leading lights in Sheffield Steel industrial history such as Benjamin Huntsman, members of the Sorby, Bailey, and Bright families have all been laid to rest here. There is no actual register of Huntsman's being buried anywhere in Sheffield, but a gravestone here gives this place more credence for his resting place than anywhere else.

The Chapel of Ease set in the Old Burial Ground on Attercliffe Common

The Old Burial Grounds' walled perimeter ended at Frank Place.

On the corner of Frank Place and Attercliffe Common was **Edwin Gowers** grocers, at **79**. **Samuel Fisher** at **77** was a fish and chip shop and in the early sixties Needhams took over this business. **Ben Welbons** fishing tackle shop came next at **75**. At **73** was **Deans Brothers**. Next door, **Keetons** which was a grocers in the late fifties at **69/71**, I don't really recall this business, but I do remember **The Victoria Wine Co Ltd.** which was at this address in the early sixties and had distinctive black and white tiling on the outside of the premises.

The Hill Top pubic house was next at **65** and this was on the corner of Newark Street. I think the Hill Top closed in the late sixties or the very early seventies. I only recall entering the pub once and the landlady threw us out for not drinking enough. We had been playing tennis and called in for a quick pint. After about 45 minutes the landlady came up to our table and seeing our glasses empty she said "are you buying any more beer". Whereupon one of the brighter members of our party said "we might, we might not". Out we went.

Across Newark Street, was **Alfred Hunts**, ice cream dealers, at **59**. I remember their son, David, who had bright ginger hair, working on the ice cream vans and being amazingly pleasant to young children who invariably tried to be smart, with remarks like "can I have crushed nuts please". If I had been working on the vans I would have obligingly granted their request. At number **51** was **Tudor Autos,** motor car body builders. Also at the same address, **51** was the **Ministry of Labour and National Service Employment Exchange (men and women)**. Next at **39**, was the **Vestry Hall**,

this housed **Doctors Jason Blyth** and **Kenneth Blyth**, a **Community Centre** and **Women's Welfare Clinic** (Family Planning).

At **33** was **Samuel Berners**, sweetshop, this was an automatic stop to purchase your 'sweets' when going to the Globe.

An old picture, 1920s?? of the Globe picture house

The Globe Picture Palace (Sheffield and District Cinematograph Theatres Ltd). was next at **17** Attercliffe Common. My mother worked here as an usherette for a short period of time.

In the sixties when the Globe closed the **Globe Service Station** was built on the same site.

Globe Service Station in the sixties

The funeral services shop of the Brightside and Carbrook Co-operative Society

The final business on Attercliffe Common is
The Brightside & Carbrook (Sheffield) Co-operative Society Limited at **3-15**.
The family who ran the undertaking side of this business, in the mid fifties, were called the Swifts. I recall Linda Swift being at Carbrook School and I am sure her parents ran the business. Below and right, are some statements from which you can judge the costs of what a Co-op funeral service would cost in around 1956.

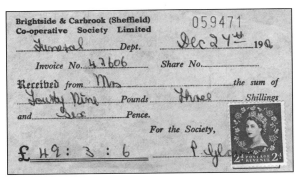

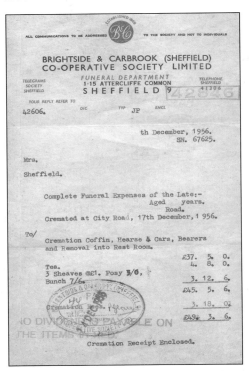

kirkbridge road to **worksop road**

The first shops on Attercliffe Road

Fairprice Fireplace Ltd, at **865** was the first or the last business on Attercliffe Road depending on which way you view it. We will continue, on the same side, upwards towards the city centre, still wandering up the 'cliffe.

I can vividly recall the following businesses trading in the mid to late fifties. Between the start of Attercliffe Road and Clay Street a mixed variety of businesses were to be found, at **863** a **Post Office**, **861**, **Browns** boot repairers, **859 Pierrepont**, greengrocer, **857**, **Harris** Confectioners at **855** and **853** was **Augustus Woodrow,** a butcher who dealt in horse flesh, a fact stated in the local directories of the day. At **851** the compulsory pub on the corner, was **The Tramcar** which was on the corner with Clay Street. Steve Otley, my grandfather's brother, could be found in this pub almost every dinner and night time session in the fifties and sixties.

The Tramcar public house

Two views of Clay Street in the sixties

The top picture showing the terraced housing, the old outside loo, and the kids enjoying their marbles.

The bottom picture showing children coming out of the corner shop.

Across Clay Street, on its other corner with Attercliffe Road, was a gents outfitters, **Newsoms.** Between Clay Street and Newhall Road there were about 15 or 16 more businesses. At **847** was **Edward Olivers** a butchers, one would have to imagine this was another of the Oliver family, who seemed, to have a butcher's shop on almost every block in Attercliffe.

Joan Liversidge standing outside Wagstaffs shop in 1980, tailors shop on the left

Ernest Wagstaff

At **841** was **Wagstaffs** sweet shop, my mother Joan Liversidge worked here for about 18 years. The owner of the premises was Ernest Wagstaff, a gentleman who was already into his eighties when I knew him. He was probably the most active octogenarian I have ever had the privilege of meeting. When he was forced to sell his shop, due to demolition, he used to go and sell his cigarettes and confectionery from the boot of his car at places like British Tissues at Oughtibridge, and at many other firms who would let him enter their premises.

In the fifties, number **839** was owned by **W Evans** who was a fishmonger, cold slabs, and smelly dead fish, not a shop you hung around for long. Many years later I remember this particular shop as a tailors, and a very good one at that. A Pakistani gentleman, I hope I have his nationality correct, was the occupant then. His daughter Shugrah was a friend of my mother's. I think she went back to her country of origin to get married and for a few years she continued to write the odd letter and sent postcards to the staff at Wagstaffs.

A couple of shops in this block, were called Whittaker, one was a florist owned by **Beatrice Whittaker** at **837** and at **833 John Whittakers**' was a fruitshop. Of the other shops I only recall two, **Gallons** grocers at **821** and **Marshall**, leather shop at **831**. Marshalls shop was a lovely place to stop and browse around. The quality, the feel and the smell of the goods that were made there were all amazing. I have a wallet I bought for a friend's 21st in 1969, I liked it so much I never gave it to him and I still use it to this day.

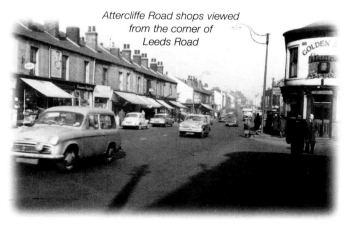

Attercliffe Road shops viewed from the corner of Leeds Road

A church parade heading towards Attercliffe Common in 1957

Gallons I remember for slightly different reasons. Every weekday dinnertime, during 1965 and 1966, I had to fetch the dinners or snacks for the staff at **Elias Bradbury Printers**, where I was an apprentice. Mrs Bradbury, the owner's wife, would not let me make a note of the staff needs. She used to say I should remember their orders in my head. I cannot say I was the brightest person at the age of 16 and invariably cocked things up. I loved the job of being an apprentice compositor but I used to worry more about that dinnertime trip to Gallons than any other aspect of my job.

At the corner with Newhall Road at **813-815** Attercliffe Road was **Brompton Snack Bar and Cafe;** this was my little oasis when leaving Bradburys at finishing time, 4.45pm. I used to have a quick drink and chocolate bar whilst waiting for the Number 5 bus to take me home to Southey Green. The bus stop was just around the corner on Brompton Road and you could keep a watchful eye on it till you saw the driver climbing back into his cab and then a mad dash was made to get on board.

Above the Brompton Road Cafe was Newhall Chambers, a series of offices, which included London and Manchester Assurance Ltd and in the mid sixties Coldwell, Williamson and Bates.

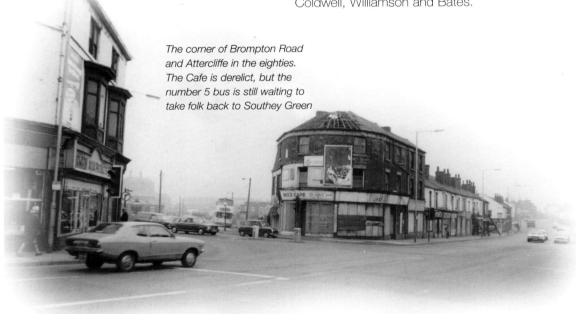

The corner of Brompton Road and Attercliffe in the eighties. The Cafe is derelict, but the number 5 bus is still waiting to take folk back to Southey Green

42

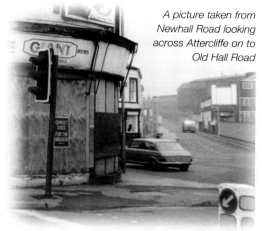

A picture taken from Newhall Road looking across Attercliffe on to Old Hall Road

After Brompton Road you came to Newhall Road, which ran from Attercliffe Road to Carlisle Street East, cutting across Alfred Road and Brightside Lane. This was another little haven for the menfolk. Four public houses on Newhall Road the **Lodge Inn** at **143**, the **Forge Inn** at **95**, the **Vine Tavern**, at **49-51** and last but not least the **Brickmakers** at **19-21** plus at **243** the McCartin brothers **Snooker and Billiard Hall**. Along with about twenty or so small shops Newhall Road was a very busy thoroughfare indeed.

On the other side of the road were Hadfields (Hecla Works), Sanderson Brothers steelworks and Millspaugh Ltd.

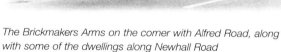

The Brickmakers Arms on the corner with Alfred Road, along with some of the dwellings along Newhall Road

The Forge on the corner of Newhall Road and Don Road

The newsagents near to the corner of Newhall Road with Attercliffe Road.

Althams tea merchants and grocers c1966

We now turn back on to Attercliffe Road and head up to Christ Church which is directly opposite Worksop Road.

Situated on the corner of Newhall Road and Attercliffe Road at **807**, was **A. Morris** paint manufacturers, at **805**, **Althams** tea manufacturers came next, another one of those shops that seemed to sell everything you could possibly need. **Taylors** tobacconists came next and at **801** was the **Brightside and Carbrook Chemist**. At **799** was **Matthews** house furnishers. I also remember this premises later as **Kitters fashions** in the late sixties. Mr Kitter, the owner, was a large gentleman who always seemed to be smoking an enormous cigar. Kitters fashion was on the corner with Vicarage Road. Roger Kitter, his son, had a

The Adelphi cinema interior

modicum of success on the local clubs' circuit and television, as a comedian.

The vicarage for Christ Church, the **Adelphi Picture Theatre** and the **Attercliffe Branch Schools Clinic** were all on Vicarage Road. The Adelphi was the only cinema down Attercliffe that had a commissioniare, a man whose nickname was "Buttons". He would roam up and down the aisle and deal swiftly with any untowards behaviour. He was only a slightly built chap, but he stood no nonsense from anyone. Any unruly behaviour at all was deemed to be an ejectable offence.

Being a regular cinemagoer to this day I now see the benefit of old Buttons.

A Mr Rowntree was the person in charge of the school clinic, a bald man with a large beard.

On the other corner of Vicarage Road, at **783-787** was the **Ministry of Pensions and National Insurance**. I do not, personally, remember Burtons being in or above the ministry premises but as you can still see the Burtons logo engraved on the upper walls of this building I think it must have been so at some time. Businesses between the Ministry and **763**, **Barclays** Bank were redeveloped in the early sixties. I seem to remember the bank and some shops being built or refurbished and slightly set back from Attercliffe Road. At number **761** Attercliffe Road was **Snelsons** radio and television dealers, **759, Singer Sewing Machines** followed by a small single storey premises, **Pierrepont** greengrocers. I remember large queues would form at this outlet even though there were five or six staff serving. It did seem a rather profitable business. Another bank, **William Deacons** came after Pierreponts, and finally **Christ Church, Attercliffe Church** make up this section.

Looking from Worksop Road across Attercliffe, Deacons Bank, Pierreponts, Singers

44

An oil painting by
D Little
Worksop Road - Brown Baileys offices
and a scammel.
The cocked hat is to be
seen on the left

A watercolour painting by **Bradbury** of the
Wentworth Hotel
Milford Street

a painting by **Rick** of the Regal cinema and Staniforth Road

*A watercolour by **Brian Smith** of the Lambpool Attercliffe Common*

Crossing over and going back to Kirkbridge Road, we start Attercliffe Road and head once again up to Worksop Road.

On the corner of Kirkbridge Road was the old **Attercliffe Sale and Exchange**. This was the second of the shops where you would try to make a killing by selling some old piece of family history that no one wanted, but you still

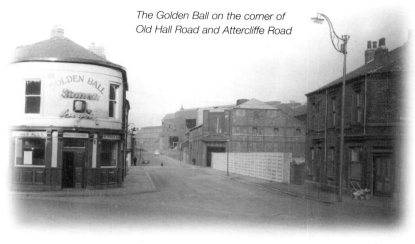

The Golden Ball on the corner of Old Hall Road and Attercliffe Road

thought may be worth a few bob, This chap would sit there and explain to you your heirloom was worth next to nowt and a few bob really was its worth. This was as much as he could possibly offer and still make a living. A few days later it was in the window for a quid or above. Next door at **866**

Children playing on an old car on derelict land off Old Hall Road

was the **Wyworry Snackbar**. A few years later, possibly in the sixties. I seem to remember it was called the **Copper Kettle Cafe**. Ernest Giles optician followed at **864/862.** After Giles's came a piece of spare land which always had an advertising hoarding positioned on it. Then came the **Golden Ball** at **838.** The 'gilded knacker' as it was affectionately known by locals was, to my recollection, a rather downbeat pub. It seemed reasonably inviting on the outside but inside it was dark and dreary. In the late eighties the pub was renamed the Turnpike and fought on against the recession for a couple of years. In 1989 there was a fire on the premises and this finally led to its closure and eventual demolition. The Golden Ball stood proudly on the corner of Attercliffe

Road and Old Hall Road for more than one hundred and sixty years. The position is now occupied by the **Don Valley Stadium,** present home of the Sheffield Eagles Rugby Club. Leeds Road came together with Old Hall Road at this point. **Brown Baileys** main entrance was also to be found on Leeds Road.

Brown Baileys melting shop

Attercliffe Baths at the corner of Leeds Road

Sheffield Corporation Public Baths was on the corner of Attercliffe Road and Leeds Road. Free entry vouchers from school, a perforated inch square piece of card, could be gained by being a good pupil for a few days. We would enter in the unrealistic hope that we might get the baths to ourselves. Invariably it was full of screaming kids, and unfortunately, sometimes people you did not wish to come across on the street, never mind the baths. The local bullies were even more scary in six feet of water than they were on dry land. On one trip to the baths, an older pupil from Coleridge Road, no names mentioned as I think I would still be afraid of him now, grabbed me from behind and proceeded to give me a life saving lesson with me being the rescued party for the full duration of my visit, 45 minutes. Being a non swimmer who just went with friends to mess around in the shallow end, this experience, was very nearly the end of my Attercliffe Bath visiting days. Occasionally I was talked into going back to the baths but I would make sure when I entered that my tormentor was not to be seen lurking, waiting to pounce.

Behind the baths on the corner of Beverley Street and Leeds Road was **Attercliffe Library**, my favourite place in Attercliffe. When no one was out playing football in the winter when the nights were drawing in, I would go and sit at one of the tables and just relax and read a book. One of my teachers at Coleridge Road School, Mr Dixon, introduced me to science fiction: The Time Machine by H G Wells. From that point onwards I was hooked on this genre and the library was where I could lay my hands on science fiction books for free. And more often than not the library was warmer than home.

Attercliffe Library on the corner of Beverley Street

The Greyhound

Back on to Attercliffe Road and the next premises to the baths was another public house, **The Greyhound**, at **822**. This pub has above its entrance a tiled picture of a racing greyhound at full stretch. The Greyhound pub is still going strong. **Bradburys printers** followed at **808.** As stated earlier, I worked at this company from August 1964 until April 1966, as an apprentice compositor. I used to spend many of my lunch breaks with a work colleague Dave Higton and together we stood with **Frank Beaumont** outside his electrical goods shop, at **806**, chatting and watching all the young ladies walk past. Well it was the era when the miniskirts were coming upon the scene. Other shops on this block before Beverley Street were: **Kirks** fishmongers, **Don Valley** cleaners, **Coombes** shoe repairers, **Jarmans** jewellers, later to become **J Dobsons** jewellers and on the corner at 792-794 was **Attercliffe Liberal Club**. On Beverley Street itself there was another club **The Attercliffe Victory Social Working Men's Club and Institute**.

At **790** was the butchery department of the **Brightside and Carbrook Co-operative**. I must admit I have great trouble bringing this premises to mind, I only seem to remember a car sales lot at this location. A couple of shops, **Laws** grocers, and **Pickerings** tripe shop came next before the **Travellers'** public house at **784**.

Dobsons, the Attercliffe Jewellers, Attercliffe Liberal Club on the corner of Beverley Street

Attercliffe Road prospering businesses in the sixties
Bradburys, Beaumonts, Don Valley Cleaners,
Coombes, Jarmans jewellers

The Travellers

Peter Swan, Sheffield Wednesday and England player, was the landlord of the Travellers' during the mid to late sixties. Swan, will probably be remembered more for being mixed up in the bribes scandal of 1963 than for his playing skills. But it should not be forgotten that he rightly gained 19 England caps and, in my humble opinion, was the best centre half to put on the blue and white stripes of the Owls. Pete was also a very good publican.

The two remaining businesses before Worksop Road were **Sam Yarwoods**, pastrycook, and **Collins** hairdressers.

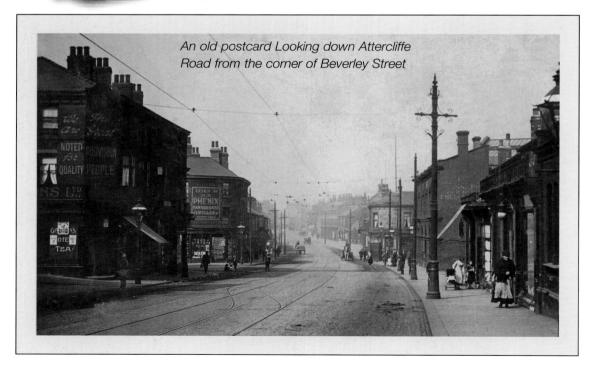

An old postcard Looking down Attercliffe
Road from the corner of Beverley Street

worksop road to shirland lane

Before we continue up Attercliffe Road, a slight detour onto **Worksop Road** is necessary, mainly because of its public houses. From Attercliffe Road to the canal aquaduct and railway arch there were six pubs in about a 200 yards stretch. On the left hand side the Omnibus, a large cream tiled

public house that was closed in the late fifties or early sixties, the Cocked Hat and the White Hart. On the opposite side the Britannia, the Cutlers and the Old Blue Bell. Part of Brown Baileys Steel Company was also on Worksop Road along with the Emmanuel Youth Club.

The Omnibus, on the corner of Worksop Road and Attercliffe Road can just be seen at the end of the row of dwelling

The Britannia Inn has a history entwined with the Sheffield tradition of steelmaking. The Britannia housed Benjamin Huntsman, the inventor of the process of making crucible steel. who fathered the steelmaking industry in Sheffield. It is said he lived the latter years of his life at these premises.

It is reputed by some, that the 24 inch high numbers/date 1772, on the side of the Britannia were made by Huntsman himself.

The Brit, Cocked Hat and the Cutlers (now Farahs) are all still surviving and seem to have quite a sizeable client base especially on weekend nights.

Shops on Worksop Road just beyond the Britannia

left:
The Cocked Hat and The Cutlers

below:
Old Blue Bell,
White Hart and Britannia,

The snooker hall above Rossingtons Bazaar

Going back on to Attercliffe Road we start with a building that is still standing proudly today.
My first memories of this building are from the fifties when it was **Boots Chemist.** It was **Rossingtons Bazaar** in the sixties and seventies and finally an Indian Restaurant which it remains today. Above this premises was **Sheffield Billiards Halls Co Ltd.**, the entrance to which was at **760**. In between at **762** was **Burgon & Son** grocers. Next was the **Coach and Horses** public house at **756**. My main memories of this hostelry was for its good pint of Double Diamond, which was the colour of strong black tea. And for the fact that we were caught playing cards with our money on the table. This practice was illegal in the sixties and the constabulary often nipped in to check the pub just to have a look around for under age drinkers and stupid gamblers, like us, who they would warn

View of Attercliffe Road taken from outside the King's Head

that next time you would be taking a walk to Whitworth Lane. It is hard to believe in this day and age but then it was enough of a dressing down to warrant a much more careful attitude to gambling in the public houses. The same policemen, who chastised us earlier in the evening, also bade us goodnight at around 10.30pm as our paths crossed again when we were making our way home. He was checking every door of all the businesses he walked past, something that I remember was common practice, for the police, in the sixties.

Coach and Horses now the Swan Hotel

The Station Hotel

At **732** was the **Station Hotel** which was built in 1833. It was a Wards public house until the Brewery closed in the nineties. The Station itself is long and narrow and is said to have been three cottages transformed into one long structure.

It was well known around the Attercliffe area that the Station had a ghost, supposedly the spirit of an occupant of one of the afore mentioned cottages who was savagely knifed to death. The public house itself is made up of two rooms, one, very small having four tables with a small serving bar area and the door leading directly on to Attercliffe Road. The other room is quite long and it was in this room that turns or acts would perform on Friday and Saturday nights in the 60s and 70s, when Attercliffe was still a thriving area. This Station was licensed in 1833 before Victoria came to the throne, but it took it another 140 years for it to get its spirit license.

Just before the station was the **Attercliffe Methodist Hall**. Whilst I do not recall this place at all, my father tells me it was not just a place for religious meetings, it also held **Gloops** club as well as boy scout and girl guide meetings. By the way Gloops was an ugly character created by the Sheffield Star, and to this day I'm not really sure what it/he/she was supposed to be. Personally, it frightened the life out of me as a kid. During the late fifties or early sixties a **Post Office**, which is still in use, was opened at this location.

A tobacconist, **Wagstaff's** was at **730**, **Harry Hewitts** hairdresser was at **728**, a butchers, **Myers** was at **726**, and on the corner of Attercliffe Road and Bodmin Street at **718-724** was **Chapman Brothers** drapers, a little later in the sixties **Matthews** furniture store was to be found at this premises.

From Bodmin Street to Brinsworth Street there were ten businesses. Unfortunately, I can

The window of Harry Hewitts Hairdressers

only recall one shop from the whole of this row, that was **Hagues** fish and chip shop which was at **708**.

Brinsworth Street came next and I will just diversify a little to inform you of a lovely little story I have heard from an acquaintance of mine, Ron Eaton. His grandmother, Mrs Lilley, lived at 17-24 Brinsworth Street and used her premises as a bed and breakfast/boarding house for the acts or turns who played Attercliffe Palace. Ron showed me a couple of books his grandmother kept at the house in the early war years 1940-1941. One was the register which contained: name, nationality, length of stay, next destination etc. and a second book was for remarks, ie "Thank you Mrs Lilley for a happy and comfortable week" you know the sort of thing. In the first book minor luminaries appear such as Beryl Reid, Norman Vaughan, Davy King and the like. An autograph collector may say the log with the signatures would be worth more in cash terms, but to me it is the other book that really hits the nail on the head about what was thought of Attercliffe. After pages of the general "lovely stay, will recommend" one act has the nerve to say what he really thinks. To be fair he still gives Mrs Lilley credit for her hospitality, but continues, "it is a great pity that the bombs, during Sheffields blitz, missed the Palace" and follows up with "what a grimy place Attercliffe really is". For the next dozen or so pages the showbiz visitors, obviously buoyed by this chap's vitriolic remarks all seem to vent their true feelings of what they think of the Attercliffe Palace as the bottom rung on the ladder to showbusiness stardom. A grand little piece of Attercliffe history. Thanks Ron.

SURNAME	CHRISTIAN NAME	NATIONALITY	DATE OF ARRIVAL. AND LAST WEEKS. ADDRESS	DATE OF DEPARTURE	NEXT WEEKS ADDRESS
Cross	Martha E. N.	British	21.10.40. Keighley	25th Oct	Barnsley
Reid	Beryl	British	21.10.40 Keighley Hippo	25th Oct	T.R. Barnsley
Barbour	Roy Jr.	British	28.10.40 Hull) Tivoli	3rd Nov	Barnsley
Barbour	Peter	British	28.10.40 Hull)	3rd Nov	Barnsley
Beck	Alma & George	British	4.11.40 Barrow	10 Nov	Chesterfield
Sheppard	Harry & Jenny	British	12/11/40 Rhyl	17/11/40	Preston
Stanton	Archie & Doris	British	17/11/40 St. Helens	24/11/40	Grand Bolton
Harrison	William	British	24th Nov.1940 Barnsley T. Royal	Dec. 1st. 1940	33 Launce St. Blackpool
Harrison	Dorothy Alexandra	British	24th Nov.1940 Barnsley T. Royal	Dec. 1st. 1940	33 Launce St. Blackpool
Dalton	Lennox	British	1-12-40 Stockton	Dec 8 40	T. Royal Barnsley
Dalton	Tony	British	2-12-40 Manchester	Dec 8th 40	T. Royal. Barnsley
Walker	Fred	British	9/12/40	Dec 15th 40	Liverpool
"	Elizabeth Mary	"	9/12/40	"	"
Golfus	Mr & Mrs Audrey	British	5/1/41. Nelson	11/1/41	London
Adams	Marjorie	British	12/1/41 Hippo Salford	19/1/41	London
Vaughan	Norman	"	12/1/41 " "	" "	Liverpool
Jones		"	1?/1/41 " "	18/1/41	Wrexham

Above: The register used by Mrs Lilley in which Beryl Reid and Norman Vaughan's names can clearly be seen second from top and second from bottom respectively.

Below: The Attercliffe Palace

To add some credence to this story, I personally, remember many years ago on television, Bruce Forsyth, Max Bygraves and Des O'Connor discussing the Attercliffe Palace and stating it was just about as low as you got before actually getting a proper job. I think they may have gone lower. Oops.

My last visit at the age of six was just before the Palace closed its doors for the last time in 1955. My trips to the Palace are now only vague memories, but what I do recall was the fire curtain full of colourful adverts and of course, the nudes. When the curtains opened on these models they stood transfixed in one pose, no movement was allowed. The curtains closed, opened again and a new pose had been struck, this continued for about 10 minutes, probably 5 or 6 poses for the audience to gawp at.

Funny how those little tit bits stick in the mind!!

The Attercliffe Palace started life as the Alhambra in 1898 and brought down its curtains for the final time, 57 years later, in June 1955. It closed with a show called Strip, Sauce and Spice. By the early 1950s the Palace like many smaller theatres was running into financial difficulties and introduced nude shows to try to keep going.

The next block, Brinsworth Street to Shirland Lane housed eight businesses. At the corner of Brinsworth Street and Attercliffe Road was the **Brightside and Carbrook Co-operative** painting and decorating depot at **688**. The others were **Bertram Plomley**, dentist, **686**, **Dennis Slacks**, bakers, **682**, **Edmands** a book library at **680**, **Attercliffe Palace, 664/678** and in the late fifties

after the Palace closure, **Brook Shaw** motor car dealers followed by a newspaper/tobacconist, **Leesons**. The **Queen's Head** was the final premises of the eight standing on the corner with Shirland Lane.

During the sixties I worked directly opposite this block of shops, at

The Co-op Painting and Decorating depot

Fred Mellings Printers. I recall fetching many a sandwich from Slacks, chocolate bars and cigarettes from Leesons and sometimes going for the odd pint in the Queens Head Hotel. The landlord of the Queen's at that time was a large Irishman named Gerry, a chap you did not mess with. One dinner time session we had the privilege of seeing Gerry throw a man out of the Queens. Nothing unusual in that, I hear you say, but Gerry bodily picked him up and launched him down the seven stone steps that led on to Attercliffe Road from the Queens front door and the poor chap missed all the steps and crashed on to the pavement. His crime was to renege on a payment for a darts match in

which he had backed himself to win. Upon losing he had refused to pay his opponent.

In stepped Gerry!!!!

The Queen's Head

Going back down Attercliffe we now endeavour to cover the equivalent stretch but on the opposite side of the road.

Christ Church, was on the corner of Church Lane and Attercliffe Road. This church was consecrated on 26th April 1826 by the Archbishop of York, nearly four years after the first stone was laid by the protestant,12th Duke of Norfolk in October 1822. The church was designed by architect Thomas Taylor from Leeds for a, then, stunning cost of £11,700. The church was damaged in the Sheffield Blitz, December 1940, and a few years later it was demolished.

Christ Church, Attercliffe

Palais de Danse

On Church Lane itself there were three businesses that I recall, **Sheffield United Tours Limited**, **Websters Furnishing Co Ltd** and in between these was the **Palais de Danse**, roller skating rink. The Palais opened in the late twenties and closed in the sixties.

We turn back on to Attercliffe Road and find **Yeomans**, tobacconists at, **721**, next came **Neville Reeds, Benefit Footwear**, followed by the **King's Head** this was also known as the Champions Rest earlier last century

One of the last beer's only houses in Sheffield. The King's Head building was used as a grocers, a earthenwear dealers, a chemist and best of all a beer house.

Some of its inhabitants are engrained in Sheffield history: The earthenware shop was run by Robert Jackson, whose son Samuel was born in the building. Young Samuel was co-founder of Spear and Jackson, the world famous tool manufacturers.

George Littlewood, whose athletics career was second to none, was a world champion endurance runner and did his training in Tinsley Park Woods, his trainer being, Thomas Chick.

On September 7th 1880 he ran, and won, a race of 406 miles' distance. His prize was a gold medal and £50 prize money. Littlewood competed in America, Australia and in Europe. He was landlord of the King's Head at the turn of the last century. Another landlord was Billy Calvert, a boxer of some repute who fought for a world championship when he took on Howard Winston in the 1960s.

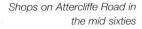

Shops on Attercliffe Road in the mid sixties

Meadows, Kings Head, Benefit shoes, Neville Reed and Yeomens tobacconists

Meadows Dairy Company Limited, butter dealers at **707**, **Naylors** Jewellers and **Stylo Boot Co Ltd,** were some of the businesses between the King's Head and **Woolworths Bazaar** which stood at **679-683**. Woolworths was one of three large department stores in this area, the others being Banners and Littlewoods. When I worked at Mellings on Zion Lane, Roger Midlane, a good friend and work colleague used to eat our sandwiches during working hours and leave our lunch break free to leisurely walk around these shops.

Between Woolworths and Zion Lane were another six or so businesses, of these I only recall **Johnsons** cleaners, **Seniors** shoe shop, and **Leslie Cass** Jewellers. I purchased my wife's 18 carat gold and sapphire engagement ring from Cass's for £28/10s/0d in Sept 1969. It would cost a bob or two more now.

Johnson Bros, Seniors, Neals, Cass, and further down you can see Woolworths Bazaar

An old picture looking down Zion lane toward Christ Church

Fred Mellings Limited, was my place of work, as a compositor, for about eight years from 1966 until 1974. The old Zion Lane Chapel, where we worked, had been transformed into a letterpress printers in the thirties.

Mellings entrance can just be seen on the left of this picture of Zion Lane

*Zion Lane Chapel
Fred Mellings Ltd
Chapel Printing
works*

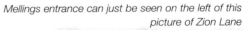

Johnson Bros, Seniors, Neals, Cass, Walkers and Tailorfit

In my old directory of Attercliffe Road the next two businesses after Zion Lane are stated as being **Kellet** laminated spring engineer, and **Brightside and Carbrook Co-op**. These two establishments purportedly covered the whole block to its joining with Baker Street.

I must be honest and say I cannot remember these shops at all. I only recall from the early sixties, **Carlines** Supermarket on the corner of Zion Lane and Attercliffe and next door was **Boots** Chemist, followed by possibly **Visionhire** and **John Temple** tailors, and on the corner of Baker Street I remember **Frankern Motors**.

Lee Frogatt and I visited John Temples shop in the latter part of 1967 to each have a suit made to measure. When I look back at pictures of Lee and myself in those suits I often wonder who they were made to measure for.

Definitely not us

Many years later, sometime in the eighties, Temples shop was turned into a massage parlour, The Omega, I believe.

The Visionhire shop

shirland lane to staniforth road

This small distance, possibly no more than 200 yards housed Banners, Littlewoods, Burgess, Burtons, Timpsons and the Astoria Ballroom. This is the area most people bring to mind when they think of Attercliffe.

We will start at the corner of Shirland Lane and Attercliffe Road. In the fifties **Talbots**, dominated the corner and **Shentalls** was next with **Scotts** hairdressers making up the three businesses before Baltic Lane.

Talbots butchers and Waterall standing at each side of Baltic Lane

Whilst I remember these shops in situ, I more readily recall a bank being on the corner and Talbots as pictured, above, filling the remainder of the block.

In the seventies, **Eric Waterall's** shop was on the other corner of Baltic Lane, 644 Attercliffe Road.

This premises, years earlier in the late fifties, was occupied by **Lee's** Tripe Shop. At 642 was **Mrs Sarah Marsdens** herbalist, This was followed by the **Horse and Jockey** public house on the corner with Baltic Road.

Across Baltic Road stood **John Banners Limited**, a large 5 floor department store that was the beacon of Attercliffe.

Looking from Sleaford Street toward the Horse and Jockey

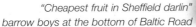

On Baltic Road at its junction with the 'Cliffe there were fruit and veg barrow boys yelling at you that no better bargain could be found in the whole of Sheffield. They traded on the roads at either side of Banners, Baltic Road and Shortridge Street.

"Cheapest fruit in Sheffield darlin"
barrow boys at the bottom of Baltic Road

Baltic Road photographed in 1963. Note the street lamp attached to the wall

Looking from Sleaford Street toward the Horse and Jockey and Banners Department Store

An advertisement in 1957 for John Banners Ltd - The Family Store

BANNERS FOR VALUE, VARIETY AND SERVICE
YOUR SHOPPING PROBLEMS SOLVED AT BANNERS.   RELIABLE MERCHANDISE
FOR YOUR FAMILY, HOME AND YOURSELF.   COURTEOUS AND HELPFUL SERVICE
The Family Store
JOHN BANNER LTD.
ATTERCLIFFE, SHEFFIELD.   *Telephone :* SHEFFIELD 41361

The Interior of Banners Department Store

John Banners money.
The old metal variety: shilling, sixpence,
1d and 1/2d, plus the newer plastic 5p

When I was a child John Banners was where I would go to get my new clothes and shoes, generally at Whitsuntide or Christmas depending on when the money lender or cheque man would let us have another loan. When you had paid off your last loan you simply got another cheque or cash slip. I recall the name of the gentleman who collected the weekly repayments from our household, his name was Mr Torr. I cannot say if he actually loaned the money or he was just the collector.

There were only about three or four outlets who would take these money slips and Banners was the store that gave the widest choice of goods. So Banners it was.

If you took a £10 cheque and bought a pair of shoes, say for £1/2s/6d, you would get £8/17s/6d back in Banners tokens (Banners money), so invariably you were tied to the shop to spend the rest. When handing the cheques or payments over to the assistants at Banners it was put into an open tube, that twisted to cover the hole, and was placed in a tube that shot it, by pressure, up to the accounts department. I remember wasting many a happy twenty minutes waiting and waiting and waiting for the return chitty so we could get started on our shopping spree.

I recall, not with any real authority, that the ground floor sold women's perfumes and clothes, the first floor men's clothes, the second floor was where you could choose your furniture and on the top floor, electrical and accounts. The basement at one stage was where the toys were housed. Many years later this was turned into a Discount Food Hall. Banners also had another shop in Sheffield, on Barnsley Road, Fir Vale.

John Banners in the seventies

Across Shortridge Street at **614/618** Attercliffe Road, was **Ernest Burgess Ltd**, tailors. I recall purchasing a suit, off the peg, at this establishment and the gentleman who served me must surely have been the forerunner of John Inmans character in "Are You Being Served". He was a local club and pub act, a comedian, who worked at Burgess's by day and did the circuit by night. I am almost certain his name was Tony Whyte. Everytime I saw Mr Whyte, who was a very dapper gentleman, he was wearing a three piece suit and had the obligatory tape measure draped around his shoulders and in general made sure his customers were kept happy.

Shortridge St barrow boy with Burgess and Littlewoods shops in background

Next door was **Littlewoods Stores** at **602/608**. This was another one of the large department stores along the 'Cliffe. When aged about 8 or 9 I used to sit at the little snack bar and have a hot Horlicks whilst my mother did her usual rummaging through the ladies garments, generally on our Saturday morning outings.

At **598** came **Paddon Watts** Chemist, **596 and 590**, **Timpson**, shoe shops. I think **Marcway** models is now occupying one of these premises.

On the corner with Staniforth Road, came **Montague Burtons Ltd**, tailors. Above this shop was the **Astoria Ballroom**.

Looking from Colwall Street across to Burgess's

"You're having that one. OK", Marcway Model shop in the seventies

To cover the equivalent stretch of Attercliffe Road on the other side would be, more or less, from Baker Street to the Carlton public house.

On the corner of Baker Street at number **629** Attercliffe Road is a large stone building which was occupied, for many years, by the Midland Bank Ltd. After the bank drew stumps and departed a few years ago, an antique dealer tried his luck, but only lasted a few years and the building is now, at the time of this book going to press, unoccupied.

Olivers butchers still going strong in the seventies

Hukins butchers, **Reed** tailors, **Brighter Homes** home decorators were next and on the corner of Sleaford Street was the **Victoria Hotel** at **621**. All I can remember of this pub is that it had swing doors, very similar to the King's Head at the top of Commercial Street. I am certain the Victoria closed in the late fifties.

Osborne carpet shop viewed from Shortridge Street

On the other corner of Sleaford Street was **Halford Cycle Co. Ltd.**, at **617/615** followed by **Easiphit** footwear, **Schweitzer** furniture dealer, **Olivers** butchers, George Oliver to be precise, **Applewhite** beer off, **Skidmore** pork butchers, **Burtons** chemist and finally **Martins** cleaners which was on the corner with Colwall Street.

Across Colwall Street on the corner with Attercliffe Common was **Wades** furnishers, at **591/597**, this address was later occupied by **R K Osborne Limited**. A couple of butchers, **Downs** and **Stensons**, a grocers, **Melias**, and finally **Bensons** hosiery at **579** made up this block of businesses before coming once again to the pub on the corner.

At the corner with Oakes Green stood the **Dog and Partridge** public house, the original Attercliffe trouble spot. My parents used to take me to the Moulders Club on a Saturday Night This was one of the few places in Attercliffe during the fifties where children were allowed into a drinking establishment, and obviously we had to walk past the Dog to get back to the Common. Invariably there was some trouble or commotion going on outside, sometimes inside and sometimes both. My father, generally with me on his shoulders, would make a point of crossing to the other side of Attercliffe Road before we came to the pub. The pub got no less troublesome as time went by. In the sixties, a teammate with Carbrook United was attacked in this pub,

Dog and Partridge

he was hit just below the eye by a woman who took off her stiletto heeled shoe and deliberately struck him in the face, causing a very nasty wound.

It served out its last few years, I would like to say trouble free, but I do doubt that somehow, having strippers, male and female, at dinnertimes and seemingly never opening in the evenings. At present the Dog and Partridge is closed.

Across Oakes Green at **569/571 Johnson's** grocers, another butchers **Thomas Austin**, and at 565 **Fragrance Cleaners**.

The area between Washford Bridge and Colwall Street was known for many years as Carlton Road. Carlton House which was off Kimberley Street was built in the 18th century and for a period of time, in the mid 19th century, was the home to Samuel Jackson, co founder of Spear and Jackson.

Carlton House

The last establishment in this section is another pub, well obviously. I used to go to

The Carlton

The Carlton at **563** Attercliffe Road on our Friday evening sojourns up Attercliffe with my teammates, when it would be a quick half of bitter and onwards to the Robin Hood. Unfortunately I made the mistake of going in this pub alone, one Saturday dinnertime, after work. I ordered a pint of bitter and stood at the bar glancing around the small room, as you do. I turned back to my pint and saw it being put down on the bar by an old man. I asked him what he thought he was doing and for a split second I thought he was a ventriloquist, a voice boomed "e's a regular 'ere thart not". I turned around to see two rather burly men sat at a table and realised the little pearl of wisdom had come from one of them. I proceeded to tell them my side of the story, that the old git had pinched a drink of my beer. I was stopped short as they stood up in unison and the landlord said "best leave, son". I did as I was bade, but I want you all to know I would have stayed and sorted it and them out, but I had a bus to catch! The Carlton still owes me a pint.

A work colleague at Mellings Printers, Roger Midlane had a similar experience in the Carlton, someone supping his beer when he turned away. Probably the same old chap. Bless him!

A busy Attercliffe Road, still a large amount of traffic on the road in the mid sixties

staniforth road to washford bridge

Before carrying on our way up Attercliffe a slight detour around the corner on to Staniforth Road.

Three places on Staniforth Road that were well frequented by myself were the **Regal**, the **Butterfly** and **Jack's Snooker Hall** which were all within about 60 yards of turning off the 'Cliffe.

The Regal was the top most of the four cinemas on offer on Attercliffe and was, I am sure, the first to disappear, possibly in the early sixties.

The **Butterfly Chinese restaurant**, built on the site of the Regal, was our final destination on many a night out around the 'Cliffe pubs in the mid to late sixties. I recall an incident on a Saturday night after a good cup win at football when we had a celebratory night out. After a pleasant evening, a Chinese meal was decided upon to bring the night to a close. About 12-14 young men descended upon the restaurant and ordered drinks and our choice of meals. A beautiful young Chinese waitress brought our food and drinks and as is the norm hovered around the kitchen entrance waiting to clear away or take further orders. After about 30 minutes, of furtively looking at her, I plucked up enough courage to go up to this young women and ask for a date or the chance to see her again. Obviously, Lee Froggatt had told everyone what I was about to do, so everybody was watching. I took a deep breath, stood, walked to where the young lady was standing and turned to look with disdain at all the glaring faces, then turned back to come face to face with a wizened old Chinaman's face. On my five second walk across the restaurant floor the attractive young waitress had gone into the kitchen and another waiter (ugly boy) had taken her place. My teammates could be heard laughing all across Attercliffe, even ugly boy laughed and I don't think he had any idea why, but he laughed. I sidled back to my seat and even when the waitress re-appeared I was too red faced and embarrassed to move.

The third establishment and the one I possibly spent more time in was **Jack's Billiard Hall**, situated just over the canal bridge on the right hand side as you go up Staniforth Road. There were two floors, the top floor had the most tables and the snack bar, but the lower floor was less frequented, so that was our more regular haunt. You would play snooker until ready to leave and then shout Jack to come downstairs and tot up how much you owed for your time spent on his tables. In the early sixties, on winter night, Jack's was possibly the one place in Attercliffe where you could go as a group and still carry on being slightly raucous. The cinemas, the herbalist and the youth clubs would tend to stop you in your tracks and quite rightly eject you and your friends if the noise level became too high.

The two banks

On the corner of Attercliffe Road and Staniforth Road were two banks, **The Yorkshire Penny Bank** at **580**, and if you did not want to deposit your money here you could always nip next door and put it in **The Sheffield Savings Bank** at **570**. These banks were built in 1905 and 1899 respectively. The old 'Penny Bank' has children's faces carved into its structure between the ground floor windows. I read somewhere that this may have been to encourage younger savers to put their money into the YPB. These penny banks were initially founded for people with only very small amounts to deposit.

Hartleys printers came next at **566-568**, Derrick Hindley and Gordon Kaye two of my old football mates worked here for many years as print machine managers. The **Robin Hood** public house followed at **548** and at the same address, using the Robin Hood yard, at the back was **Heselwood** iron and steel merchants. The Robin Hood pub was renamed Mr Smiths funbar, they should be prosecuted by the trade descriptions' people. Take it from me, no fun was to be had here! It is now a premises for swinging couples, so at least the fun levels should definitely have gone up.

Auto Clean strainers, **Bedlam** Asbestos and **Cecil Samuel** credit drapers were at **546, 546,** and **544** respectively. **Varneys** chip shop was to be found at **542**. At **534** was **Shipmans** Tool Steel & Wire Manufacturers. I can only recall this area from the sixties and then this building was trading as Spartan Steel.

The Robin Hood public house in the eighties when it was "Mr Smiths Funbar"

At the side of Spartan Steel set slightly back was the **Sportsman.**

The present building was built in the 50s to replace the original Sportsman that was bombed and destroyed in the German blitz on Sheffield in 1940. The old Sportsman was mentioned in Sheffield literature as long ago as 1888, it was then called the **Hope and Anchor**.

Spartan Steel

In the mid to late seventies my wife and I noticed this public house up for sale at a very reasonable price of £6000 and we thought long and hard about whether we should both leave our respective places of work and try the publican's trade to see if we could make a go of it. I must say with all that has happened to Attercliffe and the lack of customer base around this area I feel, for once, we made a good decision not to follow it through.

The Sportsman has closed and reopened 3 or 4 times and was for a while in the nineties a gay bar called the **Indigo**. At the time of going to press the Sportsman is still boarded up.

The Sportsman

At Number **482** Attercliffe Road, in the fifties, was **Electro-Chemical Engineering Company**. I remember the new **Attercliffe Non Political Club** (non-pots) being built sometime in the early sixties on the corner of Effingham Road. The old club is now, like the Sportsman, a gay bar, called **The Planet**. At **444** came **Hopkinsons** herbalist followed by **Hookham** motor haulage contractors which was on the corner of Lovetot Street. Across Lovetot Street was **Attercliffe Tyre Co Ltd** at number **400**, with **Sidney Smiths** grocers at **396**, followed by the **Washford Arms** at **380** Attercliffe Road and sited on the corner of Don Terrace which runs alongside the

The Washford

River Don at Washford Bridge. The Washford Arms closed as a public house in the early seventies and the premises was turned into a chip shop which is still going strong to this day.

To cover Staniforth Road to Washford Bridge on the opposite side of Attercliffe Road, we start back at the Carlton public house. At **561** was **Seniors** electricals, radio engineers, **Willerby & Co** tailors, **Gallons** provisions dealer, **Bradburys** printers, **Billingham** tobacconist, and at 551 **Boldocks** fishmongers. At this point the shops were set about 15 yards back off the road. There were possibly 4 shops in this recessed section before Kimberley Street.

Shops between Oakes Green and Kimberley Street

At **549** Attercliffe Road was **Maison Daveen**, Ladies Hairdresser, next door was **Snacks Buffet Bar** and at **545**, **General Plumbers**, on the corner of Kimberley Street was **Percy Senior** clothier.

Henry Wigfall and Son Cycle Dealers, was on the opposite corner of Kimberley Street. The rest of this block was taken up by **Wilfred Markham** Funeral Directors. A little thoroughfare, Heppenstall Lane had **B & J Plant** on its corner with Attercliffe. B & J took up a considerable area with its showroom **515**, general plumbers shop **509** and plumbers depot **503.** Nestled in

The Old Green Dragon

between all these plumbers was **Beniston** butchers at **513**. At **485** was **George Taylors** rubber cushion dealer and at **481/483 Resco Ltd** underclothing manufacturer. At **471** was the **Old Green Dragon** public house. The Dragon stood on the corner of Baldwin Street. I do not recall when the Dragon was closed or demolished but I can say for definite it was still a thriving pub in 1969/70 when we used to go and listen to people singing on the midweek talent nights. In all honesty though, I don't think they should have ever called it talent night.

On the corner of Baldwin Street was another premises for **J & B Plant**, followed by **Dowson** draper, **Broughton** tobacconist, **Drake** pork butchers and **Lambs** general store was on the corner of Armstead Road. Between Armstead Road and Stevenson Road there were seven businesses possibly the most noteworthy was at **445 Artificial Teeth Repair Company**. Another seven businesses filled the area between Stevenson Road and Trent Street. Of these outlets there were two wardrobe dealers **Mrs Fox** and **W Smith**. At **401** on the corner of Attercliffe Road and Washford Road came **Thomas Clarke and Sons Ltd** iron founders. In the fifties a public house was built on the corner of Trent Street called the **Bulldog.** Roy Davey in his book **"Pubs and People Around Sheffield"** mentions that a public house that stood here in the forties, the **Bridge**, was damaged by a bomb landing on or near Washford Bridge, a structure over the River Don.

This story is confirmed by my father who told me that he used to have to clamber across the badly, bomb-damaged Washford Bridge itself to get to his place of work (Tempered Springs). The Bridge public house continued to trade as a one storey pub until it was demolished in the late forties.

Upon this site a new pub was erected in the 1950s, and was called The Bulldog, allegedly and quite simply because the new tenant bred bulldogs as a hobby.

The Bulldog

washford bridge to twelve o'clock

It seems silly to say but the area from Washford Bridge to the end of Attercliffe Road, near Tommy Wards, was an area I only ever saw when passing through on a bus or tram. I can never remember walking through this area at all during the fifties and sixties. In fact it wasn't until after I was married in 1970 when I worked at Mellings and used, occasionally, to walk home, to Pitsmoor that I would trek from Zion Lane up Attercliffe Road before detouring at Norfolk Bridge and on to Sutherland Street.

By this time I would say nearly all the dwellings and small businesses that appear in the 1950s directory had disappeared and it seemed that on both sides of Attercliffe Road all that was left were premises occupied by a variety of smallish steel companies. Only **Tempered Springs** and **Carters**, seemed to be companies housed in buildings of any real size.

My father worked at Tempered Springs serving his apprenticeship in the late thirties, before leaving to join the navy, in 1940.

Carters' claim to fame were their world famous Little Liver Pills. I often wondered what these little pills really did!

The final leg of our trip up Attercliffe starts from Washford Bridge, or as it was more often known Attercliffe Bridge.

At **298** there was **Kennings Ltd**, motor spirit service station. Does motor spirit mean petrol? Situated at the same address was **Fisk Tyres Ltd**. **Emmanuel Church** was next, followed by **Metal Heat Treatment Ltd**, and **Beeley Foundry Light Castings** both at **286**.

At this point there are a series of companies but with no address numbers. I will just put them in the order I recall them. **George Slater**, scrap yard,

The petrol station, Emmanuel Church, and on the near side Carter manufacturing chemists

Thomas, machine tools, **National Coal Board**, Nunnery Unit, **Hardenite Steel Co**, **Thomas Andrews & Co**. Then back to numbered businesses at **180 Wincotts** furnace bricklayers, my father worked for this company for about twenty years. **Tempered Springs**, spring manufacturers were next at **162-178**. Then, of course, the statutory pub on the corner, the **Norfolk Arms**, **160** Attercliffe Road, a Tetleys House which opened in 1830, is pictured, below, standing in the shadow of its main client base, the Tempered Spring Company Limited. The public house itself was a small two roomed establishment, and it obviously catered for the steelworkers and industry in general. Like many other pubs in this area it knew it had a clientele no matter what the state of the premises,

Norfolk Arms in the shadow of Tempered Springs

Norfolk Bridge

and for many years it was in a state. After the steel industry diminished in the area around the mid 1970s the Norfolk Arms tried to survive, but it was too much of a struggle and it closed in the 1980s and the building is now being used as a sauna, the Elysium.

From the Norfolk Arms we cross Warren Street and Leveson Street, and walk under the Norfolk Bridge. Attercliffe Railway station used to be situated here. You climbed some steps at the side of the bridge. From the bridge for about two hundred yards, Attercliffe Road runs parallel with the River Don.

At **108**, **G Ward and Co**, cabinet makers, **Furnival Steel Co** at **94**, **Bentley Brothers**, motor body repairers **70-76**, **Wolstenholme**, welders and **Kirk**, engineers were at **64** and **62** respectively.

T W Wards on the banks of the River Don

The last business on this side of Attercliffe Road was **George Oxley and Sons Limited** (Vulcan Foundry) Ironfounders.

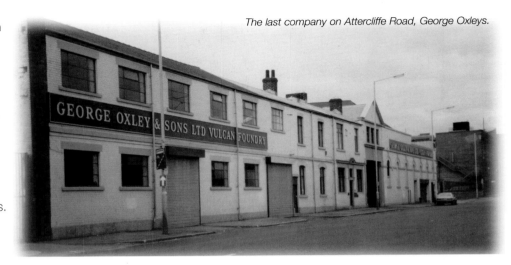

The last company on Attercliffe Road, George Oxleys.

Once again we cover the area between Washford Bridge and Twelve O'Clock Street, this time on the opposite side.

After Washford Bridge comes **John Fowler**, (Don Foundry) Ltd., ironfounders which was on the corner of Windsor Street. **Carters & Sons** (Sheffield) manufacturing chemists took up the whole of the next block until Royds Mill Street.

At **215** was **Blue Star Garage Limited**, **211 Spruce Dry Cleaners**, **209** the **Halfway Cafe**, **207 W. Kahns** a chip shop, **203**, **Storide** and **Carbon Dioxide Co**, gas manufacturers and distributors. **Royds Post Office** came next at **199** Attercliffe Road and there were four more businesses before Princess Street, **Mrs Beatrice Robertson**, wardrobe dealer was at **177**.

From Norfolk Bridge railway viaduct until the end of Attercliffe Road, I can only remember **Tunes** builders being in residence.

There were a couple of public houses in this area , they were demolished long before my time in or around Attercliffe. The **Rawsons Arms** at **161** Attercliffe Road would have been, I think, on the corner of Princess Street probably facing the Norfolk Arms.

The **Old King John**, **35** Attercliffe Road (1850s-1920s)

This public house was situated very near to the corner of Twelve O'Clock Street. As you can see from the dates it was closed about 80 years ago.

from a 1957 Local Directory

Attercliffe Road

odd numbers

Twelve O'Clock Street

Greystock Street

113	William Tune	Builders

Sutherland Street

Princess Street

177	Robertson	Wardrobe dealer
181	Moorwood	Hairdresser
183	Young	Shopkeeper
197	Walton	Shopkeeper
199	Royds Post & M. O. Office	
203	Storide Ltd.	Gas distributors
207	Kahn	Fried fish dlr.
209	Halfway Cafe	
211	Spruce Dry Cleaners	
215	Blue Star Garage	

Royds Mill Street

	Carter & Sons Ltd. Mfng. Chemists	

Windsor Street

	Fowler Ltd.	Don Foundry

Attercliffe Bridge

375-283	Brown Ltd	Laboratory Furnishers

Washford Road

401	Clarke & Sons Ltd	Ironfounders

Trent Street

Bessemer Square

421	Fox	Wardrobe dlr.
423	Franks	Newsagents
425	Squires	Shopkeeper
427	Mattock	Fruitr
429	Lawler	Boot Reprairer
433	Smith	Wardrobe Dealer
435	Nichols	Hairdresser

Stevenson Road

437	Fergione	Beer Retailer
439	Beardshall	Shopkeeper
441	Wilkinson	Fried Fish Dealer
443	Middleton	Ladies Hairdresser
445	Artificial Teeth Repair Co.	
		Dental Technicians
447	Fleming	Hairdresser
451	Letti Kan	Laundry

Armstead Road

455	Lamb	Shopkeeper
457	Drake	Pork Butcher
459	Broughton	Tobacconist
461	Dowson	Draper
463-465	B & J Plant	Plumbers

Baldwin Street

471	Old Green Dragon	Public House
481-483	Resco Ltd	Underclothing Mfrs.
485	Taylor	Rubber Cushion Dlr.
509	B & J Plant	Plumbers
513	Beniston	Butcher
515	B & J Plant	Plumbers Showrooms

Heppenstall Lane

523	Markham & Sons	Funeral Ditrs
533	Wigfall & Son	Cycle Dlrs.
537-539	Senior	Clothiers
545	General Plumbers & Glaziers Ltd.	
547	Snacks Buffet Bar	
549	Maison Daveen	Ladies Hairdrs

Kimberley Street

551	Boldock	Fish Monger
553	Billingham	Tobacconist
555	Bradbury Jn.	Printers
557-821	Gallons Ltd.	Provision Dlrs.
559	Willerby & Co. Ltd.	Tailors
561	Senior Electronic Service Ltd.	
		Radio Engnrs.
563	Carlton	Public House
565	Fragrance Cleaners Ltd	
567	Austin & sons Ltd.	Butchers
569-571	Johnson	Grocer

Oakes Green

575	Dog & Partridge	Public House
579	Benson	Hosiery Specialist
581	Melias Ltd.	Provsn. Dlrs.
583	Stenson Jr.	Pork butcher
585	Goodman & Co. Ltd.	Bakers
587	Avril's	Fancy Goods Retailers
589	Downs & Sons	Butchers
591-597	Wades Furnishing Stores Ltd.	
		House Furnishers

Colwall Street

599	Martins	Dyers & Cleaners
601	Stankler	Tailor
603	Burton	M. P. S. Chemist
605	Skidmores	Pork Butchers
607	Applewhite	Beer Retailer
609	Oliver	Butcher
611	Schweitzer & Sons	Furniture Dlrs.
613	Greenlees & Sons	
	Easiephit Footwear Ltd	
		Boot Makers
615-617	Halford Cycle & Co.	
		Cycle Agts. & Dlrs.

Sleaford Street

621	Victoria Hotel	Public House
623	Brighter Homes Ashley United	
	Industries Ltd	Wallpaper Mfrs.
625	Reed	Tailor
627	Hukin	Butcher
629	Midland Bank Ltd	

Baker Street

641-649	Brightside & Carbrook	
	Co-operative society	
653-661	Kellett & Co. Ltd.	
		Laminated Springs Engnrs.

Zion Lane

663	Johnson Bros.	Dyers & Cleaners
665-667	Senior	Boot & Shoe Dlrs.
671	Neales Ltd.	Costumiers

673	Hayman	Retail Jeweller
675	Walkers	Shoe shop
677	Tailorfit	Tailors
679 -683	Woolworth	Bazaar
685	Alexandre	Tailors
687	Cox Radiovison Ltd.	
689	Stylo Boot Co. Ltd.	
691-697	Turner	Draper
699-701	Betty	Costumiers
703-705	Naylor	Retailer Jeweller
707	Meadow Dairy	Butter Dlrs
709	King's Head	Public House
715-717	Benefit Footwear Ltd.	
719	Reed, Neville	Tailors
721	Yeomans Jr.	Who. Tobacconist

Church Lane

	Christ Church	
	Christ Church Sunday School	
747	Williams Deacon's Bank Ltd.	
753	Pierrepont	Greengrocer
755	Playfair Ltd.	Boot & shoe Dlrs.
759	Singer Sewing Machine Co. Ltd.	
761	Snelson's	Radio Supplies Dlrs.
763-765	Barclays bank ltd.	
773	Moat	Builders' Merchants
775	Reed	Tailors
777	Rose	Outfitter
779	Boston Shoe Co.	Boot & Shoe Dlrs.
781	Melias	Provision Dlrs.
783-787	Ministry of Pensions & National Insurance	

Vicarage Road

799	Matthews	House Furnishers
801	Brightside & Carbrook Co-op	
		Chemists
803	Taylor & Co.	Who. Tobacconists
805	Althams Stores	Tea Merch.
807	Morris	Paint Merch.
809	Well Done Cleaners	

Newhall Road
Brompton Road

813	Dixon	Check Traders
813-815	Brompton Snack Bar & Cafe	
813-815	Newhall Chambers	
	Dodman Caterers	
	London/Manchester Ass Co Ltd.	
817-819	Gibbs & Ward	Wollen Mers
821	Gallons	Provision Dlrs.
823	Dey	Butcher
825	Hedar	Fried Fish Dlrs.
827	Domestic Hardware Stores &	Ironmongers
829	Harris	Grocer
831	Marshall	Leather Fctrs
833	Whittaker	Fruitr.
835	Fragrance	Cleaners
837	Whittaker	Florist
839	Evans	Fishmngr.
841	Wagstaff	shopkeeper
843	Harris	Baker
845	Curson	
847	Oliver	Butcher
849	Newsom	Gents' Outfitter

Clay Street

851	Tram Car Inn	Public House
853	Woodrow	Butcher
853	Woodrow	Horse Flesh Dlrs.
857	Harris	Confectioners
859	Pierrepont	Greengrocer
861	Brown	Boot Repr.
863	Post & M.O. Office	
865	Fairprice Fireplace	Fireplace Mfrs.

Attercliffe Road

even numbers

	Oxley & Sons	Vulcan Foundry
62	Kirk & Sons Ltd	Engineers
64	Wolstenholme & Sons Ltd.	Welders
70	Bentley Brothers Ltd	
		Motor Body Builders
72-76	Bentley Brothers Ltd.	
		Commercial Vehicle Repairs
94	The Furnival Steel Co. Ltd.	
96	Sheffield Metallurgical Laboratories	
98	Mrs. C. Wood	
108	Ward & Co.	Cabinet Makers

Leveson Street
Warren Street

160	Norfolk Arms	Public House

	Tempered Springs Co. Ltd.	
		Spring Manifactores
180	Wincott Ltd	Furnace Builders
	Andrews & Co (Royds Works)	
		Steel Manufacturers
	Hardenite Steel Co. Ltd.	
		(Hardenite Steel Works)
		Steel Manufacturers
	Dyson Ltd	Ganister Manifacturers
	National Coal Board	Nunnery Unit
270	Thompson Machine Tools Ltd.	
274	Slater Ltd	Metal Brkrs.
286	Beeley Foundry	
	Light Castings Ltd.	Iron Founders
286	Metal Heat Treatment Ltd.	
		Heat Treatment Specialists
	Emmanuel Church	
296-298	Fisk Tyres Ltd.	Motor Tyre Factors
296-298	Kennings Ltd. Motor Spirit Service Stn	

Warren Street
Attercliffe Bridge
Don Terrace

380	Washford Arms	Public House
396	Smith	Grocer
400	Attercliffe Tyre Co. Ltd.	

Stoke Street
Lovetot Road

436	Hookham Ltd. Motor Haulage Contrs	
444	Hopkinson	Herbalist
482	Pickford Holland & Co.Ltd.	
		Refractory Goods Manufactors
482	Electric Furnance Company Ltd.	
482	Electric Resistance Furnance Co Ltd.	
482	Electro-Chemical Engineering Co Ltd.	

Effingham Road

534	Shipmans Ltd	
		Tool Steel & Wire Manufacturers
542	Varney	Fried Fish Dlr.
544	Samuels & Sons	Credit Drapers
546	Beldam Asbestos Co. Ltd.	
546	Auto Klean Strainers Ltd.	
548	Robin Hood	Public House
	Robin Hood Yard	
		Heselwood W. Iron & Steel Mer.
566-568	Hartley & Son Ltd	Printers
566-568	Hartley Marsland Ltd. Office furnishers	
570	The Sheffield Savings Bank	
580	Yorkshire Penny Bank Ltd.	

Staniforth Road

582-588	Burton Montague Ltd.	Tailors
582-594	Astoria Ballroom	
590	Timpson Ltd.	Boot & Shoe Dlrs.
592	Hopkinsons Ltd	Grocers
592	Farrands Ltd	Grocers
594	Dutfield Ltd	Fruitrs.

596	Timpson Ltd	Boot & Shoe Dlrs
598	Paddon Watts & Co Ltd.	Chemist
600	Hodgskinson	Shopkpr
602-608	Littlewoods Stores	
614-618	Burgess Ltd.	Tailors

Shortridge Street

Chippenham Place

620-636	John Banner Ltd	
	Drapers & General-House Furnishers	

Baltic Road

638	Horse & Jockey	Public House
642	Marsden	Herbalist
644	Lee's	Tripe Dressers

Baltic Lane

648	Scott Jn.	Hairdresser
650	Shentall Ltd	Grocers
652	Talbot	Butcher

Shirland Lane

660	Queens Head	Public house
662	Brook Shaw Ltd	Motor Car Dlrs
664-680	Brook Shaw Ltd.	Motor Car Dlrs
680	Edmands H. & J.	Book Library
682	Slack Dennis A. Ltd.	Bakers
684	Hattons	Butchers
686	Plomley Bertram	Dentist
688	Brightside Carbrook	
	Painting & Decorating Depot	

Brinsworth Street

698	Goodman J. & Co. Ltd	Bakers
700	Wiley & Co. Ltd.	Wine & Spirit Mers
702	Levison	Drapers
706	Brown	Confectioners
706a	King Coal & Co.	Coal Mers
708	Hagues	Fried Fish Dlrs
710	Ricky	Costumiers
712	Martins Ltd.	Dyers & Cleaners
714	Horswood H. & E. Ltd	Catering Serv
716	Modes E. & B.	Costumiers

Bodmin Street

718-724	Chapman Brothers Ltd.	Drapers
726	Myers	Butchers
728	Hewitt Harry	Hairdressers
730	Wagstaff	Wholesale Tobacconist
732	Station Hotel	Public House
	Attercliffe Methodist Hall	

754	Foggitt Cecil M., M.B., B. Ch.	
756	Coach & Horses	Public House
760	Sheffield Billiards Halls Co. Ltd.	
762	Burgon & Son	Grocers
764	Boots	Chemists

Worksop Road

776	Miss Molly Collins	
		Ladies' Hairdressers
778-780	Yarwood	Pastry Cook
784	Travellers' Inn	Public House
786	Pickering	Tripe Dlr.
788	Lilly Law	Shopkeeper
790	Brightside & Carbrook Butchery Dept.	

Beverley Street

792-794	Liberal Club & Institute Ltd.	
796	Jarman	Retail Jeweller
798-800	Coombes & Co.	Boot Repairers
802	Don Valley Cleaners Ltd.	
804	Kirk A. & J.	Fishmngrs
806	Beaumont	Electrical Contractors
808	Bradbury Elias	Printers
822	Greyhound Inn	Public House
824-826	Sheffield Corp Public Baths	

Leeds Road

Oldhall Road

838	Golden Ball	Public House

862-864	Gilles Ernest	Optician
866-868	Wyworry Cafe	Snack Bar
870-872	Attercliffe Sale & Exchange	

Kirkbridge Road

Attercliffe Common

odd numbers

3-15	Brightside & Carbrook	
	Co-operative Society Ltd.	
17	Globe Picture Palace	
33	Berner	Confectioners
39	Blyth Jas.	Physcn. & Surgeon
39	Blyth Kenneth	Physcn. & Surgeon
	Attercliffe Vestry Hall	
	Community Centre	
	Womens Welfare Clinic	
51	Ministry of Labour & National	
	Service Employment Exchange	
51	Tudor Autos	
		Motor Car Body Bldrs
59	Hunt	Dairyman

Newark Street

65	Hill Top Hotel	Public house
69-71	Keeton	Grocer
73	Dean Brothers	Fancy Goods
75	Welbon & Sons	Fishing Tackle Dlrs
77	Fisher	Fried Fish Dlr.
79	Gowers & Son Ltd.	Grocers

Frank Place

	Old Burial Ground	
127	Nuttall	Sports Outfitter
129	Law	Confectioner
131	Paddon Watts	Chemists
133	Wilks	Butcher
135	Attercliffe Sales & Exchange Dlrs.	

Leigh Street

137	Kirkup	Hardware dlrs.
139-141	Robinson & Son	Greengrocer
145	National Provincial Bank Ltd.	

Rotherham Street

163	Quick Press	Dyers & Cleaners
165	Boldock	Fishmonger
167	Valentine Teenage Separates	
		Ladies Outfitter
169	Baker & Son Ltd.	Ironmngrs

Bradford Street

171	Heathcote	Grocers
173	Vessey's	Pork Butchers
175	Oliver & Sons	Butchers
179	Martins Ltd.	Dyers & Cleaners
181	Laming	Baker

Steadfast Street

183	Graham Askham Motors	
		Secondhand Car Delr.
189-195	Brightside & Carbrook	
	Co-operative Society Ltd	

Berkley Street

201	Pioneer	Launderette
203	Savage & Sons	Musical Dlrs.
205	Dinitto	Jewellers

207	Langton & Sons Ltd.	Boot Mfrs.
209	Travis	Draper
211	Wagstaff	Woodworkers supplies
213	Dewhurst	Butchers
215	Hughes	Fruitr.

Amberley Street

221	Amberley Hotel	Public House
227	Peacock	Confetnr.

Tuxford Road

229	File Smiths' Arms	Public House
239	Harry marks & Co.	Outfitters
241	The Pet Shop	
243	Carbrook Cabinet & Co. Ltd.	
		House Furnishers
245	Ahmed	Grocers
247	Wickland	Jewellers
249	Skidmores	Pork Butchers
255	Spencers	Wallpaper Dlr.
257	Malloy	Grocers
259	Stokes	Drapers
263	Nimmo	Physcn. & Surgn.
271	Mansell	
273	Middleton	Tobacconist
277-283	Riley Jnr. & Son. Ltd.	
		Electrical Accessories Dlrs.
287-289	Hardwick	Grocer

Janson Street

291	Lambpool Hotel	Public House

295	Wainman	Shopkeeper
297	Glover	Newsagents
311	Robinson	Shopkeeper
315	Harrison	Greengrocers
317	Wyatt	Herbalist
319	Factory Painters	store
319	Gow Safe Board Ltd.	Store
321	Ada's	Ladies' Hairdressers
323-325	N. C. F. Ltd.	Fish mers.
333	Harry's	Hairdressers
337	Carbrook Working Mens'	
		Conservative Club
343	Quality Hardware Stores	
		Ironmongers
349	Carbrook Post & M. O. Office	

349a	Wragg Ltd.	Builders mers.
351	White	Chiropodist
	Carbrook Central Hall	
		Methodist Chapel
365	Kelly Jnr	Fishmongers
367	Pitcher	Drapers
375	Hartley	Tool Dlrs.
379	Hodgson	Butchers
381	Greensmith	Provision Dlr.
383	Marvel	Dyers & Cleaner
385-387	Hallatt	Chemists
389	Hobson	Refreshment Rooms

Milford Street

391	Thompson Jnr.	Fruitiers
393	Burton	Butcher
395	Snart	Draper
397	Ariston (Revett & Co.)Ltd	
		Tobacconists
401	Johnson	Grocers
403	Boldock	Fishmongers
405	Randall & Wagstaff	Newsagents
407	Boldock	Butcher
409	Bladen	Dressmakers
411	Metcalf R. & B.	Hardware Dlrs.
413	Websters	Boot Repairers
415	Cliffe Hairdressing	Hairdressers
419	Stamford	Fishing Tackle
421	Mann	Pork Butchers
423-433	Shaw & Son Ltd.	Outfitters
435	Lant	Fried Fish Dlrs.
437	Yeomans Jnr.	
		Wholesale Tobacconist
439-441	Gowers & Son Ltd.	grocers

Carbrook Street

443	Fearn & Son	Motor engnrs
453	Dobson Ltd.	General Dlrs.
461	Grice	Boot Repr.
469	National Union Of	
	General & Municipal Workers	
471	Shah S. & R.	Butchers
489	Wright J. & Sons Ltd.	
		Haulage Contractors

Bee Street

	Carbrook Service Station	
		Petrol Service Station
537	Carbrook Hall Hotel	Public House
	Marcroft R. S. Ltd.	Slaters
553	Oates	Physcn. & Surgn.
555	Hague	Midwife

Goulder Terrace

Warden Street

603	Earp	Grocer
607	Goudge Wm. & Son	Clog Makers
611	Hendy W. H. & E.	Shopkeepers
617	Royal Hotel	Public House

Mons Street

623	Witham	Lodging House Keeper
631	Stuart	Fried Fish Dlr.
637	Priestley	Shopkeeper

Southern Street

639	Dunn	Dressmaker
641	Triumph Libraries	
643	Francis	Ladies' Hairdressers
645-647	Fox	Jewellers
651	Union Inn	Public House
659	Boyraine	Dining Rooms
661	Salt	Confectioners
663	Slight	Wallpaper Dlrs.
665	Banks G. Ltd.	Builders
667	Benjamin	Pastrycook
669	Wade	Butcher
671	Banks G. Ltd.	Builders
673	Gleadall	Tobacconists
675	Hall	Hairdressers
677	Newbould	Ladies' Hairdresses
677a	Wilson Brothers	
		Sheet Metal Workers
679	Devonish	Fried Fish Dlr.

Weedon Street

Attercliffe Common

even numbers

Kirkbridge Road

12-14	Ferner P. & Sons Ltd.	
		Wholesale Tobacconists
16-18	Murat	Cycle Agent & Dealer
20	Taylor's	Potato Crisps
22	Sound Upholstery	
24	Cunningham	Toy Dealer

Fell Road

28-30	Clark	Grocer
32	Slack	Baker
34	Townend	Furniture Dealer
36	Caryll	Draper
38	Rimmington	Hairdresser
40	Huddart	Hardware Dealer
42	Townend	General Dealer

Howden Road

48	Kaddish	Grocer
50	Caplan	Watch Repairer
52	Holroyd J. & Co. Ltd.	
		Dyers & Cleaners
54	Race	Tripe Dealer
56	Tate	Draper
58	Dukes	Earthen ware Dealers
60	Kay	Fruitr.
62	Thorpe	Hairdresser
64	Hartle	Draper
66	Bool	General Dealer

Whitworth Lane

68	Summerhayes	Fried Fish Dealer
70	Goodman J. & Co.Ltd.	Pastrycooks
72-74	Brashaw Brothers	Newsagents
76-78	Old Gate Inn	Public House
82	Emery	Grocer
82a	Caravan Supplies	
	Timber Merchants	
86-88	Wainwright	Physician & Surgeon.
86-88	Gething	Physician & Surgeon.
90	Fane	Hardware Dlr.
92	Phoenix Cleaners	Dyers & Cleaners
94	Large	Florist
96	Hartley	Herbalist
98	Robins	Ladies Hairdresses
100	Frost C. & Sons	Ironmongers
102	Thorpe	Butcher
104	Gelsthorpe	Confectioner
106	Almey	Confectioner
108	Platt	Grocer
110	Garrett	Greengrocer
112	Buckley	Stationer
	Attercliffe Pavilion	
	Heeley & Amalgamated	Cinemas
122	Thorp	Dental Agt.
124	Brashaw Brothers	Newsagents

126	Salutation Inn	Public House

Coleridge Road
Amberley Road

130-132	Ahmed	Continental Cafe
134	Ransome	Tobacconists
136	Abbott	Wool Repository
142	Obelinde Wilson	Confectioners
144	Fukes	Tripe Seller
146	Shaw	Ladies hairdressers
152	Valentine A. & L.	Drapers
156	Wade	Fried Fish Dealer
158	Staniforth	Shopkeeper
160	Hinchliffe	Boot Repairer
162	Brown & Cawthorne	Painters
164	Jepson	Fruitr.
166-172	Dubarry	Gowns
168	Travis	Tailors
178	Nelson	Shopkeeper

Berkley Road

180-182	Parkin	Pawnbroker
186	Austwick	Fried Fish Dlr.
188	Beadman	Draper
190	Ludbrook	Ladies Hairdresser
192	Rutherford	Confectioners
194	Shentall Ltd.	Provsn.

Belmoor Road

198	Northern Vision Co. Ltd.	
		Television & Radio Supplies
200	Heathcott	Dentist
202	Toone	
206	Pearson	China Dlr.
208	Flather	Fried Fish Dealer
210	Cutts	Grocer
212	Barker	Corn Dlr.
214	Maher	Ladies Hairdressers
218	Wagstaff	Woodworkers' Supplies

Terry Street

Carbrook Elementary schools

282	Botros	Physician & Surgeon
286	Sayles	Confectioners
288	Logan	Fried Fish Dlr.

Carltonville Road

290	Mawson & Sons	Boot Repairers
292-298	Cosy Furnishing Co.	
		Furniture Dlrs.
300	Gallon's Ltd.	Grocers
302	Carrigan Jnr.	Pet Stores
312	Simpson E. & B.	Drapers
314-316	Bricklebank	Confectioners
318	Wistow	Fruitir.
320-324	Sullivan Ltd.	Cycle Dlrs.
326-328	Whyman	Grocer
330	Pashley	Leather Dlr.
332	Bennett	Butcher
334	Smith	Motor Cycle Accessories

Goulden Place

336	Green	Photographer
338	Porter	Grocer
340	Brown	Butcher
342	Broughton Inn	Public House

Broughton Lane

366	Stoppard	Draper
368	Lockwood	Plumber
370	Hewitt	Baker

Clifton Street

		372
372	Stenton M. & Co.	
		Ale & Stout Bottlers

Newton Terrace

St. Bartholomew Church
Pheasant Recreation Ground

| Pheasant | Public House |

British Thomson Houston Co Ltd.
Metropolitan -Vickers Electrical
Ward Thomson W. Ltd.
Scrap Iron Dealers

Carbrook Elementary School

The Pheasant Inn
(now The Stumble Inn)

The Adelphi, Vicarage Road

John Banners

The Norfolk Arms pub, standing in the shadow of Tempered Springs Limited

The old Boots building at the corner of Worksop Road

The Regal Cinema House on Staniforth Road